Praise for Thom's workshops and books:

"I discover something new about myself every time I reread one of Thom's books. He has a gift for saying in a sentence or two what some writers say in ten! Thom's words are straight to the point—and go straight to my heart, where they can do the most good. Thanks, Thom!"

—Janet LaLande, Mauldin, SC

"As Bill Wilson, cofounder of Alcoholics Anonymous, said: 'The secrets of the universe are shrouded in simplicity.' Thom taps into those wonderful secrets!"

—Dan Mason, Boulder, CO

"Thom delivers completely serious material with a surprising and wonderful sense of humor. More succinctly, *Thom delivers.*"

—Pam Noble, Boone, NC

"Thom's a magician. He transforms confusion into clarity."

—Robert Stepbach, Nashville, TN

The Self-Forgiveness Handbook

A Practical and Empowering Guide

Thom Rutledge

New Harbinger Publications, Inc.

Also by Thom Rutledge: *Simple Truth, If I Were They,* and *Practice Makes Practice* (audiotape). For a brochure, call (615) 327-3423

Publisher's Note

This publication is designed to provide accurate and authoritative information in regard to the subject matter covered. It is sold with the understanding that the publisher is not engaged in rendering psychological, financial, legal, or other professional services. If expert assistance or counseling is needed, the services of a competent professional should be sought.

Distributed in the U.S.A. by Publishers Group West; in Canada by Raincoast Books; in Great Britain by Airlift Book Company, Ltd.; in South Africa by Real Books, Ltd.; in Australia by Boobook; and in New Zealand by Tandem Press.

Copyright © 1997 by Thom Rutledge
New Harbinger Publications, Inc.
5674 Shattuck Avenue
Oakland, CA 94609

Cover design and illustration by Lightbourne Images © 1997.
Text design by Tracy Marie Powell.
Edited by Farrin Jacobs.

Library of Congress Catalog Card Number: 97-66077

ISBN 1-57224-083-0

Printed in Canada on recycled paper.

New Harbinger Publications' Web site address: www.newharbinger.com.

10   9   8   7   6   5   4   3   2   1

This is for Jack Loyd Rutledge and Mary Kate Rutledge.
To Dad, for teaching me the importance of self-forgiveness.
To Mom, for conspiring to bring me "out of my shell."

We are not in control of life, and no matter how hard we try, the caprices of nature will win out over man. We can never predict what the outcome of an encounter will be. We can, however, exercise some control by participating in the process of our lives.

—Arnold R. Beisser, M.D.,
A Graceful Passage

There is a big difference between being in control and being in charge.

—T. R.

Acknowledgments

Thank you to my friends who have let me know all along that I am loved and appreciated. Thank you to Carol Beck for a year of collaboration on *Getting Unstuck*, to Judy Lynn for the timely hand off, and to my ever present "guardian angels," Serenity and Silven. As always, thank you to Trish Sanders. Thank you to my clients, for trusting me with your stories, and for letting me play a part in your important lives. Especially thank you to Sharon for being my first self-help reader those many years ago.

Thank you to Melody Beattie, for your generosity and for the practical and magical work that you are doing. You are spinning in a circle and clapping your hands, aren't you?

To my editors at New Harbinger: Thank you to Farrin Jacobs for your keen eye for consistency and detail, and for treating my work with such respect. Thank you to Kristin Beck for inviting me to create *The Self-Forgiveness Handbook*, for your wise counsel when I needed it most, and for working with me to create the illusion that this isn't work. To everyone at New Harbinger: you could not have made this any easier. (Maybe this *isn't* work.)

Last, and most, thank you to my wife, Dede Beasley—this time for the tangible service of becoming my on-site, though at times reluctant, editor. This one would not exist without you.

Contents

Introduction

Forgiveness is a concept more often associated with spirituality than with psychology, or at least that's how it used to be. Increasingly—over the past twenty-five or thirty years—the line of demarcation between spirituality and psychology has blurred. For the purist from either discipline this may be disturbing. The traditionally trained psychotherapist's world is contaminated with the introduction of spiritual concepts (especially those that defy rational explanation) such as forgiveness, soul, and God. For the deeply religious, the insistence on scientific principle associated with psychological theory, not to mention the tendency to not necessarily honor mother and father, can be offensive.

In as much as the two disciplines can still be distinguished from one another, this is a book of psychology. Herein we will examine the psychology of the relationship of the Self with the Self. For some readers, this will quite naturally involve their spirituality, but there is no prerequisite belief system to benefit from The *Self-Forgiveness Handbook.* All that is required is a desire to feel better about yourself and your life.

Too often, self-help books dwell predominantly on the explanations of how we became so ... well, in need of self-help books, and then devote only a few chapters (toward the end of the book) about how we might recover from our now well-understood dysfunction. I want *The Self-Forgiveness Handbook* to be of practical use to you beginning with page one, chapter one. I want this book to be a box of tools you can learn to use—with practice—to make a real difference in your life.

Certainly, it is important to understand how we got from *point A* to *here*. After all, those who do not remember—*and understand*—the past are doomed to repeat it. I think you'll find plenty of explanation within these pages about what makes someone need a book on self-forgiveness. But there is no need to put off the work of change to the final chapters. We can learn to understand ourselves *while* we are learning how to heal. In fact, considering the negative bias that most of us have toward ourselves, it's difficult to imagine how we can become objectively understanding, let alone empathic, until we can at least learn to stop attacking ourselves at every turn.

In a way, learning self-forgiveness is the classic human search for identity. As long as we remain in hiding from the so-called negative aspects of ourselves, we remain incapable of embracing *all* of who we are. When we consider only certain of our human characteristics acceptable, we have no choice but to remain fragmented, experiencing ourselves as less than whole. And since rejecting certain aspects of ourselves does not exorcise them from our personalities, we find ourselves in a stagnant pool of guilt (for having such unsavory traits) that, left alone, will become at least the *toxins* of self-distrust and dislike, and possibly *the poisons* of self-disgust and hatred.

In one sense, all of this may come to pass due to a sort of collective ignorance, a void of essential information in our society. Sure, there are many negative, not to mention untrue, things we are taught to believe as we grow up. And destructive, false beliefs will need to be confronted and transformed. But none of these may prove as harmful as one big missing piece of developmental information: in our society, historically, we have not been taught the importance of maintaining a positive, loving and respectful relationship with ourselves. In fact, many of us have been actively discouraged from such a self-compassionate state, learning instead that to care for ourselves is selfish.

If we were not taught this essential component of good mental health—*that self-love is good and necessary*—it is for one reason: those who taught us could not teach what they did not know. There is no master plan for one generation to destroy the next; it's a matter of legitimate ignorance and/or inadequate application of knowledge.

If you take the risk of believing this to be true and decide that you can learn to forgive yourself, there will be many obstacles along the way, but none as daunting as those that you will discover within your own consciousness. Some beliefs you will gladly release, and others will be strangely difficult to let go of. This book will provide *a quality set of tools* (instruction manual included) for the task of identifying and confronting those internal obstructions.

At the blatant risk of mixing metaphors (I'm certain that I will eventually have to attend Analogies & Metaphors Anonymous) this book is also intended to provide a *practical map* to help you navigate your way from *here* to *wherever you choose to be.*

How to Get the Most Out of This Book

The Self-Forgiveness Handbook is presented in four parts. Part 1 provides what I consider to be the essentials for your self-forgiveness toolbox—the hammer, pliers, screwdriver, and wrench, so to speak. They will help you explore your personal thoughts and feelings about self-forgiveness. Part 1 ends with what some of my clients have called my "sermon" about *the healing power of awareness.* (When we can learn to slow down our thinking enough to take a more accurate look at what is going on around us and within us, everything changes. Amen.)

Part 2 introduces you to the seven components of self-forgiveness. Chapter 4 makes the introductions—Reader, these are the Seven Components; Seven Components, this is the Reader—and the subsequent chapters guide you in an exploration of each component. The response I've received from clients, workshop participants, and readers is that once this material is experienced, it becomes impossible to maintain an exclusive hold on your old negative self-image.

I think it works something like the "Hidden Pictures" game in the children's magazine, *Highlights*: You search and search and search for the image of the shoe, and you can't find it anywhere, at any angle. You've already found the duck, the thimble, the umbrella, and the puppy, but no shoe. Then, just when you are about to give up, your gaze relaxes, you sit back, and there, clear as the sky on a cloudless day, right in the middle of the big tree is the shoe. Once discovered, it becomes impossible to not see the shoe. And so will be your experience with part 2 of this book; you will no longer be able to escape your new awareness of your *committee,* your *should monster,* and your *decision maker.* And you will be stuck with the ability to recognize when you are giving away, or throwing away, your personal power.

Part 3 is a natural extension of part 2. These chapters identify common problems encountered when applying the seven components to day-to-day, "real world" life. Better yet, these chapters also suggest solutions to those common problems.

Part 4 is a bit of a departure—from the rest of the book as well as from the average self-help book—at least in how it's presented. Each section is a brief essay addressing—or posing—some question related to living a life of self-compassion. These essays were fun to write, and I hope that you will *enjoy* reading them. I am a card-carrying, charter member of the If You Don't Have a Sense of Humor, You Had Better Get One or You Are in Big Trouble Here on Planet Earth Club. I can find no where in my policy and procedure manual that says that even as we struggle to free ourselves from the tyranny of self-criticism, we can't have some fun along the way.

Part 4 is also a departure in that it dabbles in topics that are probably beyond the scope of this book. But I have never tended to color inside the lines and I don't believe that we can effectively discuss the subject of forgiveness without at least acknowledging the philosophical and spiritual implications.

Keeping a Journal

A little writing can go a long way as you explore your relationship with this powerful and elusive thing called forgiveness. Hopefully, what I (and others) have to say on the subject can be useful, but it can only be so to the degree that you are committed to remaining aware of what you think, feel, and believe. Your experience is what counts. Keeping a free-flowing journal is a tangible way of tracking and enhancing your experiences along the way.

If you don't already keep a journal, and even if you think it wouldn't make that much difference, I strongly recommend that you find a notebook of some kind—one that you like the look, size, weight, and feel of—and write in it as you read *The Self-Forgiveness Handbook*. Use your journal to do the writing exercises throughout the book, but don't stop there. Don't just take your direction from me. Your greatest wisdom, your greatest authority is not in me, not in this book. Nor will you find it in any other teacher or book. *Your truth is inside you*, and putting pen to paper when you don't have the slightest idea what might come out is an invitation for that truth and wisdom to emerge. An honest journal will always reflect that you are a work in progress—as are we all.

Here's a helpful hint about *The Self-Forgiveness Handbook*. Parts 1 and 2 will be most useful if read in sequence; these chapters are the foundation for your daily practice of self-forgiveness. But read parts 3 and 4 in any order you wish, whenever you feel the need for a little reinforcement. These chapters are like golf clubs: Choose the one you need depending on where you find yourself along the fairway.

Think of your journal as a workbook. Don't treat it too gently; don't be afraid to scribble in it or write in the margins. A journal is your work space, and it has only one purpose: to record *your* thoughts and *your* feelings—the positive and the so-called negative, the vague and the precise, the understandable and the confusing. These are all parts of the same whole: You. The totally acceptable, forgivable, and responsible you.

PART I

The Essentials

Our capacity to make peace with another person and with the world depends very much on our capacity to make peace with ourselves.

—Thich Nhat Hanh,
Living Buddha, Living Christ

1

What Self-Forgiveness Is
and What It Isn't

First, this is not a book about playing God. I have a good friend, a devoted Christian, who (when she heard the title to my new book) told me that I was going to be "treading on shaky ground." Initially, I was surprised by her response, but as we talked I came to understand that her belief—and therefore objection to my book—was that only God can forgive. But the exploration of all the philosophical and theological questions that raises is a whole book in itself.

If your religious or spiritual beliefs are similar to my friend's, I encourage you to think of *The Self-Forgiveness Handbook* as a guide to help you learn how to effectively *receive* forgiveness. What we are given, from God or from each other, is of no use unless we can learn to accept the gift(s). Those of us who would read (or write) this book will have at least one thing in common: we have all had difficulty accepting gifts, be they compliments, attention, love, or peace of mind. Most of us cannot trust good things to be genuine, or if we accept that they are genuine, we don't trust them to last. Of course this doesn't even touch upon the question of whether or not we feel we deserve the good things.

Consider the various dangers: the danger of seeking something you are sure you don't deserve; the danger of gaining something you will certainly lose; the danger of believing the best of yourself while still falling short of your personal expectations; the terror of genuinely accepting your human imperfection, letting go of the dangerous double standard by which you measure only yourself.

This book is about facing these dangers, daring to tread on that shaky ground—and living to tell the story. To open yourself to forgiveness is a frightening proposition. But remaining closed to forgiveness is not such a great option either.

The bottom line is, learning to forgive yourself is not for the faint of heart. To learn—and maybe one day to master—forgiveness and compassion as a way of life, you will need plenty of willingness to take risks, an excellent sense of humor, enormous portions of persistence, and plain, old-fashioned guts. The good news is that I will help you to discover and enhance these and many other necessary tools along the way.

If your experience with religious or spiritual beliefs has been harsh or frightening, and is contributing to a negative view of yourself, try approaching this material as an aid to detoxifying from archaic beliefs that depict you as, somehow by your very nature, sinister and undeserving. Such beliefs only serve to terrorize and paralyze; they do not pave the way to a life of serenity and personal acceptance as they claim.

What Self-Forgiveness Is

A common fear—and criticism of self-help psychology—is that self-forgiveness is a snazzy, politically correct, socially acceptable way of letting ourselves off the hook by avoiding accountability and personal responsibility. This is absolutely not true. In fact, as we will explore throughout this book, the more powerful and accurate definition of forgiveness is quite the opposite; self-forgiveness is the natural starting place for anyone who wants to lead an ethical life as free from hypocrisy as is humanly possible.

Think of it this way: When I was a kid, my father owned a dry-cleaning store. As an adolescent, I drove his delivery truck, picking up and delivering dry cleaning all around the small town where I grew up. In essence, I drove my Dad's truck around town, working to meet the needs of other people, my Dad's customers. Was my father selfish for taking excellent care of that truck? Was he being selfish to make sure its tank was full, that the oil was changed on schedule, and that the tires were aligned?

Of course not; my Dad's priority care of that truck was not about being selfish. It was about being smart. Without regular, quality maintenance, the delivery truck would eventually require much more time and attention, not to mention money, than he could afford. People are the same way.

Self-forgiveness is that regular maintenance that keeps us on the road. The self-forgiving person is not—as many believe, or at least fear—a selfish person. It is the person who remains stuck in self-doubt and self-condemnation who will lead the more selfish, less productive life. As a psychotherapist, I have learned this lesson well. The better I take care of myself, the more effective I will be with clients and workshop audiences. When I have a noisy, neglected engine rattling under my hood, I will be distracted and unfocused on the work at hand. When I "run out of gas" I won't be able to show up (mentally). Self-forgiveness keeps us from being stuck; it keeps us moving.

What I Believe

Let me tell you what I believe about forgiveness, and in particular, self-forgiveness. First, I believe that all growth moves from the inside out, and that our repetitious, and very human, attempts to resolve problems from the outside in are just what (on closer examination) they appear to be: *backwards*.

I believe that in years past if I were to love my neighbor as myself, my neighbor had better watch out.

> The first part of any conflict that I must resolve
> is that which is between me and me.

I believe that self-compassion is our first nature, and that excessive self-criticism and self-condemnation are a learned second nature. I believe that forgiveness—of ourselves and others—is not so much something we do, as it is that natural state when we are not holding on to old resentments, pain, and guilt. I also believe that resentments and grudges I hold against myself are every bit as destructive as those I harbor for the fellow down the street.

I believe that living a life of self-compassion has nothing to do with being selfish, or in any way excluding others. I believe that the first step to giving is receiving; that when we are genuinely self-forgiving, the benefits automatically (or with minimal effort) spill over into the lives of others. When we practice genuine self-forgiveness, we will naturally live according to a positive value system that includes respect for—and a desire for—the well-being of others.

I believe that in order to practice genuine self-forgiveness, we must accept full responsibility for who we are and what we do. Accountability is a requirement, and perfection is not even an option.

Finally, I believe that living a life of forgiveness, attending to daily life from the inside out, is the most energy efficient and most productive way to live. I believe that self-forgiveness is essentially inseparable from self-respect and self-responsibility.

What This Book Is and Is Not

In no way is this book an exhaustive and comprehensive study of forgiveness. As you read, bear in mind that these are one man's ideas and beliefs about forgiveness. This material is based as much on my experiences in learning to forgive myself as it is based on my teaching and clinical experience working with clients and workshop participants.

I have never trusted anyone who claimed to have the ultimate answers, and so my promise (and a sort of disclaimer, I guess) to you is that I will not claim to have *the* answers. I sincerely believe that all any self-help book, workshop, or psychotherapist can do is offer support ("You are not alone"), guidance ("Have you ever tried going down this road?"), validation ("You have a right to be in charge of your own life"), and positive confrontation ("Like it or not, you are in charge of your own life").

Like good psychotherapy, I want your experience with *The Self-Forgiveness Handbook* to be collaborative. Take what is helpful; leave what is not. But I encourage you to take time with the ideas and the exercises that follow. Try them on—as opposed to viewing them from a safe distance. Then if something doesn't fit, leave it. But if something does fit—be it shoe or otherwise—it's yours. And it will be your choice to wear it or not.

And please don't be afraid to argue with and question this book. Allowing the more restless, even rebellious parts of yourself to participate, as you will read about later, is an important part of learning how to forgive yourself. In many ways, we have learned to accept only select aspects of our personalities, and to reject others.

For example, "I'm okay as long as I'm doing something helpful for someone else, but it is selfish of me to pursue my own interests. The anger that I feel is wrong. I should be happy and grateful."

In my book, *every part* of you is welcome. Come one, come all.

Moving Toward Self-Forgiveness

Throughout many years of involvement in the process of personal growth—as a psychotherapist, as a client in psychotherapy, and as a self-help explorer—I have returned again and again to one central awareness: The key to genuine, long-lasting change lies not in the resolution of any particular circumstance, but in developing the ability to forgive oneself.

As a psychotherapist I probably spend 80 percent of my time redirecting clients' attention from the *content*, or circumstances, of their lives to the *process* of their relationship with themselves. It is the proverbial

---

Journal Exercise

What I Believe

At the top of a page write, *What I Believe about Forgiving Myself*. Then make a list, each time completing the sentence *I believe.* . . . Remember to let the associations run free. Write whatever comes to your mind without judgment—as much as that is humanly possible. And don't be concerned if you discover seemingly conflicting beliefs. These are very common, even useful, as you will see in chapter 6.

Your page will look like this:

What I Believe about Forgiving Myself

I believe _____

I believe _____

I believe _____

Etc.

---

choice between giving someone a fish and teaching someone how to fish. I can choose to approach my clients as a *collection of problems,* and set out to help solve those problems one by one, or I can approach my clients as *problem solvers,* and enter into a collaboration with them to improve their ability to solve their own problems. The latter has always made much more sense to me.

And of all the possible problems that problem solvers might encounter, there is one that seems to rise above all of the rest again and again: inappropriate and excessive self-criticism.

The Attentive Supervisor

Imagine that you and I are sitting in a room together and that I give you a task to perform; let's say the task is to complete the journal exercises in this chapter. As you begin, I lean in close over your shoulder, watching your every move. As you attempt the written task, I talk to you constantly, critiquing everything you write as you write it. I sigh heavily to express my disappointment. I clear my throat, obviously casting doubt on the sentence you've just completed. I remind you that you are probably not doing the exercise correctly and that you never have been any good at following directions, not to mention (but I do mention it) that you're not a very good writer and, while we're on the subject, don't forget that your handwriting is horrendous.

If the task was difficult to begin with, my "attentive supervision" will make it impossible. If the task is simple to begin with, my oh-so-helpful sounds and comments will make it far more difficult and complex than it needs to be.

Does any of this sound familiar? If so, it could mean that you've had a boss, a teacher, a parent, a friend, or a spouse like this. It could mean that you were taught to think of God like this. It very likely means that with or without outside assistance, you have tended to treat yourself in this constantly critical way. Sure, you may discover that you need some help with the original task, but you really can't know that until there is a significant change in your style of supervision.

In the simplest terms, that is what I do for a living: I teach people how to respect, protect, support, and even like themselves. And when that is accomplished (which is no small task), there are not many problems that cannot be solved. It's amazing how much you can get done when you are not having to look over your shoulder every other minute to see if that bully of a supervisor is coming.

> When we let go of the constant attempts to solve the *content* of our lives, and attend to the important *process* of how we treat ourselves and each other, we have a real chance for peace of mind.

The key to quality, lasting change is the presence of self-compassion. With that awareness as a starting point, over the years I have distilled into seven categories what I have come to consider the *basic components of self-forgiveness*.

The best part is that these seven components are not specific to any one problem area. If you are depressed, if you are anxious, if you are concerned about addictive or compulsive behaviors with food, drugs, alcohol, relationships, and so on, the components act as a map that can guide you to the information and insights you will need in order to face and resolve your problems. These are fishing lessons. What you decide to catch is entirely up to you.

Respecting Yourself

Going toe to toe with your problems (many of which you may have been sidestepping and ducking for years) is a frightening prospect. But with "map" in hand, plus the lessons you will learn from this book, a

---

Journal Exercise

Hopes and Fears

Make a list of some of your hopes, and the fears that accompany them.

---

tangible sense of hope will join your understandable fear. And hope and fear are not, as they may initially appear, opposites. They are, instead, old buddies—traveling companions. You will seldom find one without the other.

The seven components are also a viable set of tools for *maintaining* your successful changes. Forgiveness is never a one-time event; if it does not become a way of life, it is nothing. But when you learn to live a life of self-forgiveness, everything changes.

Specifically, self-forgiveness will allow you to gather your dreams, your desires, and your courage to live the life you choose to live, the life you want to live. But what do you want? This is not necessarily an easy question to answer. If you have grown up learning to value being hard on yourself to the point of self-induced martyrdom or self-condemnation, it will not be surprising to find that the idea of "what you want" was swept under the rug long ago.

A friend of mine offers an interesting explanation for this problem from a developmental vantage point: Children are not welcomed into the world and brought up with enough curiosity from the adults around them. My friend says that there are essentially two opposing metaphors for parenting:

1. Children are clay, and parents are the sculptors. A parent's job is to mold the child into the person the parent believes it is best to be.

2. Children are seeds, and parents are the gardeners. The job of a parent is to care for the environment in which the child will grow—providing the proper conditions for "the seed" to grow into whoever he or she is.

The lack of curiosity adults have about who children are is an inadvertent, but habitual, expression of disrespect. (Respect being defined

---

Learning self-forgiveness will change you from the inside out, creating a powerful ripple effect.

> Open-minded curiosity about another person's perspective is a powerful expression of respect.

as the conscious recognition of another's individuality.) The sculptor-parents (and other teachers) interact with children predominantly in one direction: parent to child, teacher to student. Genuine curiosity is missing, or at least in short supply.

Consider the alternative: Adults who accept responsibility for creating and maintaining a safe and ethical environment in which children can experience permission and freedom to discover for themselves who they are, what they enjoy, where their abilities lie, and what they want. Parents and teachers secure enough in themselves to have faith in their children, and who can approach child rearing with curiosity, wondering with enthusiastic interest, "Who will she be?" or "What will he be interested in as he grows up?"

In this kind of healthy environment, children learn tolerance for imperfection (theirs and others); they learn to take appropriate risks in their efforts to explore the world around them; they learn to succeed; they learn that when they fail, there is no need to surrender their self-esteem. This is the natural state of a child. With self-forgiveness, we will rediscover that natural state in ourselves.

Facing the Obstacles

For all of your potential, there will be many obstacles along the way. Fear of the unknown and a sense of not knowing what you want are only two examples. *But you can do this.* I have. And I have witnessed many others do this work and reap the rewards.

When in doubt, think of the wonderful movie, *The Wizard of Oz* (1939). Dorothy, the Scarecrow, the Tin Man, and the Cowardly Lion combined their strengths to overcome whatever was put in their path by the Wicked Witch of the West. Along the way, each of the travelers faced a sense of hopelessness, and when they did, the others were there with the encouragement needed to keep the hope alive. Ultimately they succeeded in finding the Wizard. And when they did, they discovered that what they were seeking, what each of them wanted more than anything, had been a part of them all along.

Self-forgiveness is like searching for the Wizard: when you get there you will know that you have always had a brain, a heart, courage, a

> Children are seeds. And seeds are pure potential.

Journal Exercise

Off to See the Wizard

Answer these questions to the best of your ability. Your answers can be in the form of a paragraph, a list, a poem, a story—whatever form feels right for you.

In what ways were you brought up by "sculptor-parents"?

In what ways were you brought up by "gardener-parents"?

Are you more of a sculptor or a gardener in your relationship with yourself?

What makes you curious about yourself?

What do you want from the Wizard?

home—whatever you want more than anything. It's right there inside of you. (You don't have to believe me now. Just keep reading.) And we are each other's Dorothy, Scarecrow, Tin Man, and Lion, here to remind each other to keep hope alive.

2

Self-Forgiveness and
Personal Responsibility

The yellow brick road may have been a romantic journey, but it was not an easy one. The Wizard has the power, as we all do, to point out what is already true. He does not have the power to make true what is not. I do not claim Wizard status, but very often, as a psychotherapist, my job boils down to just that: pointing out to my clients what is already true, what they have not been able to see from their perspective. Often, to make this point, I will move my eyeglasses to the top of my head, look straight at my client and say, "I can't find my glasses and I have looked everywhere."

Certainly, a large part of the road to good mental and emotional health is learning ways of thinking and behaving that are new to us. We must do this learning—a lot of which is *unlearning*—in order to live more effectively in our day-to-day lives, especially when we decide to define "effectively" as something more than the never ending pursuit to please others. Contrary to popular belief, we don't have to change ourselves in order to be good, deserving people. The challenge here is learning to *recognize* the good and the deservingness that inherently exists. The Scarecrow never really needed a brain; he needed credible, external validation

People with low self-esteem are so ready to be wrong. If something happens within a hundred-mile radius of us, we find a way to take the blame. "It must be me," we automatically assume.

If we are in conflict, and I am me, and you are you, then I must be wrong . . . somehow.

But . . . there is one subject about which people with low self-esteem adamantly refuse to admit being wrong. That subject is low self-worth. To this belief—that we are wrong, bad, or "less-than"—we hold so tightly that we couldn't possibly have space or energy for anything new and radical like feeling good about ourselves. Never.

The truth is you are not bad or "less-than." And you are wrong far less often than you have previously believed. But when it comes to this belief that you are worthless . . . Admit it! You're wrong!

of his already-existing, fully functioning brain. The same is true for you and me.

Check Your Perceptions

Have you ever known a woman who is convinced that she is ugly, or at least not very physically attractive, when the obvious truth is that she is beautiful? For the past six or seven years I have been working with young women with bulimia and anorexia. These young women experience drastic distortions in their self-perception, believing beyond all doubt that they are fat, ugly (many will describe themselves as "disgusting"), and worthless, when in fact they are slim (at least), attractive, and highly creative, productive people.

One lesson I learned quickly in working with clients with eating disorders is that telling them *the truth* about themselves, especially their physical appearance, carries no weight. (I suppose that pun was intended.) In fact, to do so, more often than not, is quite counterproductive. If I tell a thin woman with bulimia that she is the opposite of fat, the result will most likely be that she digs in with her opinion even deeper, defending her perception that she is overweight. The lesson learned: I can't do it for them.

The body- and self-image distortions presented by people with eating disorders are a magnified, exaggerated version of something that is true for us all. None of us see ourselves entirely accurately, and no one can convince us that something about ourselves is true when we believe strongly that it is not so. Validation will be accepted only when there is a corresponding internal awareness. For my clients with eating disorders, that usually comes in the form of their acknowledging that it is *possible* that their perceptions are not accurate. (That may not seem like much, but for them, it is extremely difficult, and is indicative of a milestone in their recovery.) Likewise, in order to benefit from the external validation of your family, peers, or caregivers, you must become *willing to be wrong* about your self-perceptions. No one can do that for you.

No Reprieve from Responsibility

A criticism that frequently comes up in my line of work is that I'm letting people "off the hook," offering a reprieve from personal responsibility. Interestingly, this criticism often comes from clients and workshop participants themselves. I generally have two responses to this concern:

1. I agree that learning self-forgiveness *must not be mistaken for a free ride*.

2. The criticism itself is often *an expression of fear*.

Ultimately, it's not about blame, it's about responsibility.

No Free Ride

There is no doubt that the trend in psychotherapy and self-help organizations known as the *codependency movement* (at its peak in the mid to late 1980s) produced some abuses: in brief, we were told to find our inner children, which we did. The problem was that no one had much to say about who was going to parent these inner children.

Eventually, most professionals involved with the codependency movement, and more and more of the lay support organizations, caught on. In the early '90s I started facilitating a one-day workshop called *Discovering the Parent Within* that became quite popular. Essentially, the basis of this workshop was to encourage people to take the best the codependency material had to offer (which was quite good in my opinion), but never to forget that the purpose of the inner child metaphor is to create a healthy self-to-self relationship in order to assume our rightful position as self-caring adults who accept full responsibility for our choices. In other words, *use* the metaphor; don't get lost in it. In order to be self-forgiving, some part of the self has to be responsibly taking charge.

An Expression of Fear

The idea that I'm going around "letting people off the hook" of personal responsibility, beyond being a reasonable concern, is an expression of fear—*fear of the unknown*, what else?

As you will read about in later chapters, most people are accustomed to motivation by pressure, specifically the pressure created by the threat of heavy duty self-criticism and/or the criticism of others. When we start talking about self-forgiveness and living a life based on self-compassion, the objections move to the foreground: *If people are self-forgiving, what's to keep them from doing anything they want and then justifying it in the name of self-compassion?* The fear is that it is the self-criticism that has kept us in line all these years; we fear that we cannot be trusted on our own.

The answer to this question, of course, is that there is nothing to stop people from using this information for self-justification. Doing so, however, entirely misses the point of true self-compassion. These people are not self-forgiving; they are self-serving.

Two Kinds of Guilt

To be self-forgiving is not to abdicate having a clear conscience. If you let yourself off the hook for things you need to be held responsible for, then self-forgiveness loses all credibility. On the other hand, if you hold yourself responsible for things that are beyond your control, or if you are incapable of letting go of the guilt once the necessary lessons have been learned, and the corrections made, you will become less, not more, effective in leading a responsible life.

Think of it this way: You are a swift sailboat, moving across the water with a strong wind. You are making excellent forward progress. Suddenly, a member of your crew drops a big, heavy anchor attached to a strong chain that is in turn attached to your boat. With sails full out, and an excellent wind, what happens to your sailboat now?

If the chain is long enough so that the anchor hits bottom, then the anchor is likely to become lodged in a permanent position, and your boat will be capable of nothing better than going in circles around the heavy anchor. If the chain is not so long, or if the water is very deep, then your boat will continue its forward progress, but at a significantly slower pace, as it drags the heavy anchor behind.

Guilt is the anchor, and when the anchor is dropped, it is important that you recognize it as such, stopping to take inventory of your situation, including your own behavior. When you have erred, you must accept responsibility and attend to your mistake. Once that is done, however, your job is to pull up the anchor and proceed forward. That is, I suppose, a nautical description of how natural, healthy guilt operates. This guilt doesn't hurt; it helps. It "keeps you honest," demanding your attention when you stray from your own value system.

What is not so effective is a captain who believes that once an anchor is dropped, it stays put. This is neurotic, unhealthy guilt—guilt that is hurtful instead of helpful; and guilt that demands attention constantly becomes a major impediment to any forward progress. Often, this type of guilt is only loosely (or not at all) associated with current circumstances. This guilt does not make you more responsible; it leaves you more self-absorbed, with your sails flapping in the wind.

Confronting the Truth

Self-forgiveness is based on the truth, not on some fantasy that everything we do is perfectly all right. A significant part of the truth is that *we are*—like it or not—*imperfect beings*. Ironically, to not accept our imperfection as fact will inevitably lead us to victimization, the natural result of endless attempts to achieve something that is impossible. As victims of self-perpetuated (if not self-induced) perfectionism, we are once more the sailboats weighed down by an untold number of heavy anchors.

> Perfectionism is a state of perpetual victimization.

And so, the first truth to confront is that you and I are imperfect, and that will not change. When we accept this truth, we will be more capable of accepting responsibility for what is appropriate and deflecting what is truly not ours to be responsible for.

Another truth is that the best way to be fully available to others is to take excellent care of ourselves, or in our nautical terms, to mind our own anchors. Only when we learn the difference between neurotic guilt (multiple anchors in the water) and natural guilt (attending to each anchor in turn, and raising the anchor when corrections have been made) will we become fully responsible for ourselves. In this way, personal responsibility is necessary for genuine self-forgiveness, *and* self-forgiveness is necessary for genuine personal responsibility.

May the circle be unbroken.

3

The Power of Awareness

Awareness is underrated and too often overlooked. You might say *we are unaware of the power of awareness.* Sometimes we are afraid of awareness; we are afraid of what we will see or what we might learn about ourselves if we open our eyes wide and take a good look. We are afraid that all of the negative things we have thought about ourselves will prove to be true. Or we are afraid that if we look too closely, we will find nothing, just a big, blank, empty space. No wonder we so often prefer our faithful blinders, or better yet, blindfolds.

The problem with the blinders and blindfolds is that any sense of security or comfort they offer is, at best, temporary, and more than likely a booby trap. As tempting as it is to look away from a reality that will predictably be painful to face, clear, honest awareness is necessary for anyone who is serious about transforming long-standing self-critical habits into self-compassion. Awareness is a powerful healing agent. Awareness is such a significant part of the foundation for change that when we avoid it or minimize its importance, whatever we build is destined to tumble. Simple, honest awareness—that is not misused to bolster self-condemnation—will set the wheels of change in motion. It is not all there is, but it is the starting place, *the very foundation of lasting change.*

Before we take one more step in our search for self-forgiveness, we must slow down—come to a complete stop if necessary—and do whatever it takes to rescue the healing power of simple awareness.

Avoiding Awareness

We are programmed to take any piece of new awareness and move instantly to take some action. "Do something. Quick. . . . Something! Anything!" our insides scream as we become uncomfortable with what is going on around us, or inside of us. It's not that you or I necessarily experience these thoughts consciously (although we sometimes will); the trigger to take immediate action is more of a reflex—completely self-contained and automatic.

This kind of impulsive movement will remove us from any awareness we are beginning to experience, resulting in more of a medicating or distracting behavior than a positive, productive action. We actually move into the action to *avoid* the awareness, rather than moving into action as a natural part of expanding our awareness.

And without a full experience of what is going on "in the now," it is predictable that we will be ill-equipped to get where we want to go. For instance, if I want to get to New York City from where I sit right now in Nashville, Tennessee, I not only need to know where New York is on the map, I had better know where Nashville is. Knowing exactly where I am right now will make all the difference in my travels. Criticizing myself for being in Nashville when I want to be in New York will be of no use. *Avoiding* the knowledge of precisely where I am certainly won't help.

And yet, we continue to make decisions, again and again, without enough accurate information. Besides being afraid of what clear awareness might expose, we are also impatient. We don't like to move slowly, even when it is in our own best interest. The internal critical messages push us—for them we can never do enough, we can never be enough, and we can never move fast enough.

If you decide to take the advice of this chapter to practice slowing down, you can bet that your internal criticism will escalate. Stand firm. Help is on the way.

The Best Advice: Slow Down

"Slow down"—more times than not, these two words are good advice. But this is far easier said than done. For instance, give this a try: As soon as you finish reading this sentence, put the book down, close your eyes and take five full, deep breaths . . . Slowly.

Whatever just happened for you is a perfectly acceptable experience. Maybe—even probably—you haven't stopped reading to experience the five deep breaths. Maybe you did, or you plan to later, or as soon as you find out why I am asking you to do such a simple, silly thing. Maybe you have a *Reflex Rebel* like I do that says, "I don't have to. You can't make me." No matter how you responded to my suggestion, you have the opportunity to increase your self-awareness. For example, you might be thinking, "I didn't realize how rebellious I become in response to such simple, innocuous suggestions."

When you get the hang of it, everything becomes a potential source for increased awareness. It's kind of like Martha Stewart using everyday, household items to create . . . whatever it is that Martha Stewart creates.

Journal Exercise

Taking Inventory

Stop and take five deep breaths—slowly. Then describe your experience by writing an inventory of everything you became aware of. Include physical discomfort and sensations, emotions, rebellious and cynical thoughts, self-deprecating thoughts, hopeful thoughts. Write *everything* down. Most of your inventory may not be anything you didn't already know, but you are probably not used to thinking of this information as potentially valuable.

When (or if) you stop to take five deep breaths, you will have an experience of self-awareness. And again, even if you refuse to do the exercise, as long as you are paying attention, you will have an experience of self-awareness. It's as simple as that. It may or may not *feel* simple.

Taking five deep breaths is an excellent technique for checking out the level of your anxiety at any given moment. It's a way to stop and listen to your fears. Again, no wonder we are so impatient: we are trying to outrun our fears, when the better approach is to move toward our fears, gathering all of the information that we can.

Awareness of the Negative

You must learn to become more fully aware of the world around you and the world within you. Be aware of your own tendency to interpret your environment in self-critical ways. Be aware of your tendency to convert what is happening within and around you into self-indictment, implicit and explicit messages about how you should do, feel and be different. You might even write these critical messages down in your

---

Walk toward your demons—they take
their power from your retreat.

journal; acknowledge their realness. The fear of bringing these negative thoughts into the light results from a belief that they are true. Facing this inner negativity is essential to achieving the goal of self-forgiveness.

> Being safe and feeling fear are not opposites.
> One of the great challenges of self-forgiveness
> is finding our way to feel safe enough to
> finally experience our deepest fears.

Simple awareness is a powerful and necessary tool for facing your inner negativity and the many other challenges that lie ahead. Obviously, waiting around for the fear to subside, or for someone to offer enough reassurance to make the fear go away, will not work. Making a decision to step into increased awareness must initially be a leap of faith.

Patience and Commitment

Please do not misunderstand any of this to say that taking action does not have its place in healthy lives, because it certainly does. Awareness and action, as Forrest Gump might say, go together like peas and carrots.

But our abilities to use awareness are atrophied—they need work, need to be exercised. Ask anyone who has made a comeback from serious physical injury and they will tell you that no matter how simple the rehab exercise program may look, it is hard, hard work. Rehabilitating your use of awareness is no different. No matter how simple it seems (and therefore how you *should* be able to master it in a day and a half according to your self-criticism), mastering the use of your own simple awareness is hard, hard work and will require from you a strong commitment and an abundance of patience.

Don't worry too much if your commitment and patience cupboards are bare. These are qualities of self-compassion that we will be working on all along the way. For now, just put one foot in front of the other and ... follow the yellow brick road.

Experiment

One-Breath Meditation

I am by nature, restless. Having made many attempts at establishing a daily practice of meditation, and always feeling like I didn't have time for it, I hit upon the idea of a *one-breath meditation*. I knew that my "not having time" was just an excuse, although it was an accurate expression of my priorities. The one-breath meditation took away any and all excuses about time. After all, who can claim that they don't have time to take one breath?

The One-Breath Meditation: Before leaving your house each day, sit down in a comfortable position. You don't need a designated place, just sit anywhere comfortable. Keeping your back straight (plain old good posture), slowly take in one full breath. Imagine yourself filling up with clear, clean, fresh energy throughout your whole body. At the end of the inhale, wait to exhale for about three seconds. Then exhale, releasing your breath slowly, imagining that you are clearing your body and mind of all that is used, stale, or toxic. Just when you believe you have completed the exhale, push a little more air out of your lungs (you'll be surprised how much is left in there). Lastly, while you are resuming your normal breathing, remain still for about five more seconds.

That's all there is to it. I dare you to tell me that you don't have time.

Points of Reference
(The Essentials)

- Think of yourself as a problem solver, not as a collection of problems.

- The key to creating real change is learning how to treat yourself with genuine respect.

- Awareness is a powerful healing agent. Facing inner negativity with full awareness is the first step to developing a positive self-image.

- Fears are full of lessons. Be determined to learn, and face your fears head on.

- When in doubt: slow down, take a deep breath, look around. Since doubt is not rare, neither should your moments of quiet and reflection be.

Copy this list into your journal. Add your own points of reference. Pack all this to take with you into Part 2 . . . and into the rest of your life.

PART II

The Seven Components of Self-Forgiveness

*Forgiveness can be more than an act
of the moment; it can be a way of life.*

—Whitley Strieber,
Breakthrough

4

Introducing the Seven Components

Seven is no magic number, although it does seem to pop up frequently in self-help books these days (Stephen Covey's *Seven Habits of Highly Successful People* (1989), Deepak Chopra's *Seven Spiritual Laws of Success* (1994)—both excellent books, by the way). Disassembling self-forgiveness into seven components is merely a way to organize this information so that it is *easy to remember* and *accessible to practical application*. This second purpose is extremely important because no amount of intellectual understanding (alone) will bring about the change that you want. If this information is not put into practice, it is useless.

Three Metaphors

The Components As Tools

It is the *daily application* of your intellectual understanding of this material that will steadily erode your automatic self-critical thinking, opening the space where compassion for yourself belongs. I cannot stress enough that the seven components of self-forgiveness, and the other material in this book, are tools. *You* are the craftsman.

The hammer, screwdriver, pliers, nails, and so on that are in my toolbox in the garage right now are of no use to me until I decide to pick them up and put them to use. For me that has often called for a decision to learn how to use the tools. The tools of self-forgiveness are no different. If they are not used, the toolbox just gathers dust.

The Components As a Map

Now that we have looked at the seven components as a box of tools, let's consider them as a map—a map that can guide you from where you are to where you want to be. Like the five stages of grief described many years ago by Dr. Elizabeth Kubler-Ross, the order of the seven components represents a general progression, but by no means an absolute linear process. Each person's experience will be unique when it comes to the practical application.

However, you'll find that one component does naturally lead to the next so that when you are feeling stuck, you can retrace your steps to discover the obstacle or obstacles in your path. Accurately identifying an obstacle, otherwise known as *defining the problem*, is an obvious, but frequently overlooked, step in problem resolution. So try imagining the components as the map that will guide you back to the main road leading to the *Land of Self-Compassion*.

The Components As Clothing

As a psychotherapist, I have never been one of those quiet, nodding, beard scratchers, nor have I ever been particularly comfortable being the one to tell people what is wrong with them. The first approach seems like a rip-off to me, and the latter disrespectful of a person's individuality. I tell clients that I am more the "fashion consultant" kind of therapist—that is, I will listen to them and respond with information that I believe may be helpful according to what I have heard. I want them to "try on the information" to see how it fits. It may be a perfect fit, or it may be in need of minor or major alterations, or it may not fit at all. I want to participate actively—good therapy is collaborative—but I don't want to categorize people or assume that I know what is best for them to do. I like being direct by telling my clients exactly what I think about "the fit," but I remain committed to remembering that what someone takes from the process of psychotherapy is *never* my call.

The same is true for what I write—I guess this is kind of like mail-order catalog clothing. The seven components are designed for the general population, or at least for those of us who tend to be pretty hard on ourselves. I want you to try this material on, wear it around, even experiment with your own unique "alterations." If and when it fits, wear it.

The Seven Components

So, whether the seven components are tools or a map or clothes off the rack—or a metaphor of your own invention—here is a brief overview to get you started. I encourage you to take a little time after reading this chapter to write your initial responses to the components described. Initial responses are very often full of uncensored—and therefore valuable—information about your desires, hopes, and fears.

One: Acknowledging the Committee

First, you must admit that you are never just one person. The *myth of singularity* (the belief that sanity and intelligence are demonstrated by having *only one opinion* or *only one feeling* about something) must be exposed for the culprit that it is. You'll learn that by identifying and understanding the various "personalities" within one personality, you actually feel more together, more sane—even before problems are solved. To be self-forgiving, you must adopt this more realistic model for how you process information. The bottom line is we all talk to ourselves and we need to get better at it.

Two: Identifying the Should Monster in Charge

Once the multiple nature of your consciousness is clarified, normalized, and accepted, the next logical step is determining who is in charge of the "committee within." Usually a powerful little character that I call the *Should Monster* is at the helm, directing your life with intimidating *shoulds*, *oughts*, and *if onlys*. Here you can begin to see that the distribution of power within your committee is grossly out of whack.

Three: Understanding the Should Source

You need to know how the self-criticism develops. By exploring "the lessons" learned in childhood, you can begin to answer the persistent, nagging question of "Why am I the way that I am?" The purpose of discovering the source of the shoulds is not to assign blame to your parents, other family members, or other sources of authority, but rather to begin the essential process of *letting go of self-blame.*

Four: Discovering a Decision Maker

Now that you are a crowded conference room ruled by a relentless tyrant from known origins, your distress may make more sense, but why do you probably feel worse? It's easy to become overwhelmed with this scenario. The next question to ask is, "Where is the hero of my story?" By heightening awareness of *who you are not* (the Should Monster in particular), you begin to discover more of who you are, and subsequently who you will need to be in order to take charge of your own life: A Decision Maker who can listen to the entire committee and make decisions based on the information available, rather than on a policy of perpetual self-indictment. You need a Decision Maker who is powerful *and* compassionate, a combination many people are not accustomed to.

Five: Building the Power

As difficult as it is to face your own destructive self-criticism, often the greater challenge is in creating and empowering the new Decision Maker. At the outset of this work, it's difficult to find someone in there who will even claim the authority to forgive you. You cannot "just say no" to the negative without investing in an alternative. And like it or not, that alternative is to do whatever it takes to become a powerful, self-caring adult, a Decision Maker in charge of your own life. To be in charge does not mean that you control everything; it simply means that you accept the responsibility for learning how to be the very best adult in your own life—a frightening prospect for many. But it can be done.

Six: Learning to Succeed

The so-called *fear of success* is most often a thinly veiled version of the *fear of failure.* It's not success that people fear as much as it is the responsibilities and expectations that go with it; we are afraid that we won't be able to handle it, that success will only set us up for a bigger fall. In the case of self-forgiveness, the challenge is to change long-standing beliefs about yourself, and in order to accomplish this you must learn to

- Swim against strong currents of habitually negative thinking

- Separate the experience of positive thoughts about yourself from the threats and internal put-downs that often accompany them

- Come to accept yourself as an attractive, independent, and competent person

Sometimes this component presents the greatest challenge of all. But if you can't see yourself in terms of success, then it will be difficult to feel good enough about yourself to forgive.

Seven: Practicing, Practicing, Practicing

None of this will work until you can accept this simple truth: Perfection is not one of your choices. Practice makes ... practice. As long as you insist on striving for the impossible, you will remain a loyal subject to your Should Monster. Only through learning to accept—and even to value—your imperfection (otherwise known as being human), will you discover the freedom to enjoy this constant learning experience called life. The ultimate goal is to live a life in which self-forgiveness is a daily practice—like exercise, meditation, or brushing your teeth.

Journal Exercise

First Impressions of the Seven Components

Which of the seven components is the easiest for you to relate to? Which is the most difficult?

Write about any *hope* that reading this chapter has given you. Then write about the *fears* this chapter has awakened in you.

Remember: this is just a first run-through of the seven components. Next, we will dive a little deeper into each of them ...

5

One:
Acknowledging the
Committee

We are not alone. And this is not a reference to the possibility of our making some new extraterrestrial friends. The fact is, not one of us can honestly claim to be completely singular in nature, even though the unspoken assumption is that we *should* be. We are supposed to have *one opinion* or *one feeling* at a time. Experiencing seemingly conflicting opinions or emotions is regarded as problematic—as in *confused* (at best) and *insane* (at worst).

A classic example of this is the treacherous dilemma of "Do I feel guilty or do I feel angry?" We are taught that in order to be angry, we must be able to prove beyond a reasonable doubt (or sometimes beyond *all* doubt) that someone has done us wrong. I may feel angry, but if the other person involved did not have malicious intent, or if for any reason his or her actions were understandable, then I have no right to feel angry. Immediately I return to my rightful place: guilt. What we are not told is that it is more realistic to acknowledge that there are times when we will feel both anger *and* guilt—simultaneously.

Another common example: If I'm feeling dissatisfied or frustrated, then I'm ungrateful. Again, the two frequently coexist—I can be grateful for all of my good fortune *and* dissatisfied with some aspects of my life. In each of these examples, the underlying erroneous assumption is that in any given circumstance, there is one right way to feel. We simply will not fit into these restricting either/or boxes. There isn't just one right way to feel or think. With Component One you will learn to recognize the *many* voices, the various inner characters who make up your personal committee.

The Myth of Singularity

Have you ever felt incompetent or crazy because you couldn't decide if you thought *this* or thought *that*, or if you felt *this way* or *that way*? By defining ourselves as singular in nature, we inevitably become trapped in these either/or dilemmas. Rather than being taught to use introspective awareness to develop a more accurate self-definition, we are taught—by example mostly—to deny an expanded (or multiple) view of our personalities, and to embrace a standard that is essentially impossible to meet: *The Myth of Singularity*.

> The answer to most either/or questions is . . . YES.

Consider the various ways the Myth of Singularity is imposed on us: Many adults with families, in midcareer, are still trying to figure out what they want to be "when they grow up," as if there is only one right answer. We are taught to seek that one person with whom we are "meant to be," while all that we might be learning about the hard work of a successful relationship is neglected.

Virtually any decision we face is framed in an either/or context. The more important the decision is to us, the greater the pressure to "get it right." How often have you experienced almost total mental paralysis in the face of an important decision?

Thinking of ourselves as singular in nature is quite simply an ineffective frame of reference from which to live our lives successfully and happily. It's a set-up.

Talking to Yourself

A friend of mine, a teacher, used to begin his communication course by asking the students, "How many of you talk to yourselves?" He tells me that usually about three quarters of the students raised their hands, some more slowly and reluctantly than others. After all, admitting that you talk to yourself could be an indictment of insanity, and that is certainly no way to impress your teacher on the first day of class.

My friend would then follow his first question with, "How many of you have just asked yourselves, 'Do I talk to myself?' and replied, 'No, I don't think so.' or 'Even if I did talk to myself, it wouldn't be any of his business'?"

The obvious point being: we all talk to ourselves. Anthony Robbins, author of the best-selling *Awaken the Giant Within* (1991), points out that talking to ourselves—specifically, asking ourselves questions and answering those questions—is how we think. With this in mind, the question of sanity, and of plain old effectiveness, becomes more a matter of *how* we talk to ourselves, rather than *if* we talk to ourselves.

> We all talk to ourselves. And we all answer back.
> We just need to get better at it.

Think "Relationship"

Confusion will reign for as long as you continue to think in terms of, and believe in, the Myth of Singularity. Ironically, clarity will begin to set in as soon as you think of yourself as multiple in nature. As strange as it may sound, considering the relationships within your one consciousness is the gateway to self-responsibility, self-compassion, and increased self-understanding. By identifying and eventually accepting this more realistic model for how you process information, you establish a context in which any problem can be solved. You will learn to problem solve in terms of a continuum of effectiveness rather than the black-and-white model of right or wrong, good or bad. Rather than getting bogged down in the either/ors, you can put more effective questions to your committee of internal voices. For example, given a choice between plan A and plan B, you ask the committee, "What are the benefits and the drawbacks of each of these plans?"

The next time you face a conflict—small, medium, or large—ask yourself this important question: "What part of this conflict is between me and me?" This question is not intended to deny any external elements of your dilemma; your problem will very likely involve a relationship with another person or with a particular circumstance in your life. But by beginning with this question, you will be practicing the principle recently illuminated by Stephen Covey (1989) of *putting first things first*. And when we put first things first, I believe that we will be honoring another important principle of effective self-care: Growth always moves from the inside out.

A New Definition for Sanity

Without really giving it much thought, most of us accept the Myth of Singularity as at least a part of our definition for sanity. That is, until we are introduced to the possibility that talking to ourselves is normal, maybe even helpful. Then a conversation such as the following might ensue:

New Me: I'm beginning to believe that there is more than one of me in here.

Old Me: Sit down and be quiet. Nobody asked you. There is only one me, and it's me.

New Me: But I spend a lot of time confused and feeling bad. I think that the idea of focusing on the relationships within myself really might help.

Old Me: You are so gullible. Don't you know that you can't believe everything you read in those silly books of yours?

New Me: Have you noticed that we are having a conversation *right now*?

Old Me: (long pause) Sit down and be quiet. There is only one me, and it's me.

The better definition for sanity begins with an acceptance of our multiple nature. This does not mean that we are all diagnosable as having multiple personality disorder. It simply means our conscious minds are learning to look both ways: to not only look *out* into our world of relationships, but also to look (and listen) *inwardly* to the very important, and largely overlooked world of inner relationships. In fact, once you can recognize this more realistic model for understanding how your mind works, you will have a new, improved definition for sanity, a definition that has more to do with accurately identifying what is really going on as opposed to keeping up appearances for the outside world.

Speaking from experience; given an either/or choice, I would rather feel sane than appear sane. The good news is that I (and you) can have both . . . most of the time. (*Can't I? Yes, I think so. Oh yeah, I'm not so sure. Who are you? You don't recognize me? You're me! Well, that's a given . . .*)

From Strange to Calm

I have been working with individuals and groups for many years now, helping them to identify the various voices and personalities within their one consciousness. I sometimes have to remind myself of how strange this sounds to someone just learning about it. It has become an automatic way of thinking, about myself and about others. For me—and many others I've known—acknowledging and respecting the many aspects of my oneself has been a calming influence, a way of making sense of myself. And when we can make sense of ourselves, we can more readily practice self-forgiveness in any given moment and as a way of life.

Say Hello to the Gang

Hold on to your hats. Once you begin to look inside for these relationships, especially the ones that are giving you trouble, you just might feel like the dam has burst. Awareness gathers momentum like a snowball down a steep hill.

In the introduction I described the "Hidden Picture" game from the children's magazine *Highlights*. You look and look but you can't find that shoe in the picture, or the bunny, or the spoon. But then you see it. There the shoe is, plain as day, right in the middle of the tree trunk. Later, your friend is searching for the hidden pictures, but she can't find that darn shoe. You look over her shoulder, and there's the shoe, obvious to you now, right in the middle of the tree trunk. You cannot *not* see it. And the same will soon be true of your friend, whenever she finds the shoe, or when you point it out to her.

New awareness is like finding the hidden picture. Once you identify something within yourself, such as the simple fact that you talk to yourself, you may forget to look for it, but when you do look, you cannot *not* see it. You can sweep new awareness under the rug, but you cannot ignore the lumps in the rug.

If it does feel overwhelming at first, think of it this way: The committee members within you have been operating all these years without anyone on the outside being aware of them. Now all of a sudden, you, the bright young conscious mind (let's be optimistic) walk in. The conference room is probably a wreck; just think of all the unresolved material that is stacked on the tables, in the corners, on the chairs, next to the coffee pot—probably a fire hazard. The room is hot and stuffy; there hasn't been fresh air in here since . . . well, maybe ever. One or two big shots are standing at the end of the long conference table; one in particular does most, if not all, of the talking. (You'll read about this big shot in the next chapter, so stay tuned.) A few others may be sitting at the table, persistent ones, trying to make their thoughts count. And others have given up, a couple of them playing cards in the corner; most of them sitting along the wall with their heads down. At least one of them is sound asleep.

The big shots are not going to be happy to see you. After all, they have all the power. They don't want to be interrupted. The others, at the table and scattered around the room, will not likely respond to your entrance one way or the other. They don't have a clue who you are and what you have come to do. For that matter, you may not know either.

But there you are. You have found the hidden picture. And this ragtag group in the dark and dusty conference room is *your committee*.

For just that one moment when you open the door, everything stops, and they all look right at you. Say hello to the gang.

Eavesdropping

For now, the most important work you can be doing is gathering information—finding the hidden pictures and becoming an observer of your inner relationships. Remember the power of awareness from chapter 2 and practice using that power as you silently watch and eavesdrop on your committee. Listen for the arguments that will break out from time to time among committee members. As your eavesdropping skills improve, expand your knowledge of how your committee works. Be creative; have some fun. Try writing a dialogue between two committee members, or even a mini-play involving several of them.

Don't worry about mastering this for now. Much more will be revealed that will help you fine tune your eavesdropping skills. Just be sure to bring Component One with you when you feel ready to move on to Component Two.

Journal Exercise
Naming Your Committee

Take a few minutes to visualize your committee, then compose a paragraph or two about what you see and experience when you open the door to your conference room.

Designate a page in your journal to be a roster of your committee members. Write a few down now and add more as you become aware of them. Let your imagination be your guide, remembering that there is no wrong way to do this exercise, no matter what the big shots within tell you. As an example, here is a partial list of some of my more permanent committee members:

The Should Monster	The Skeptic	The Rager
The Pouter	The Carefree One	The Loner
The Creative Guy	The Avoider	The Rebel
The Entertainer	The Logician	The Teacher

Remember that your human nature is multiple, not singular; so if you experience your committee in more than one way, do the exercise in more than one way. Believe me, there will be plenty of room for everybody.

Points of Reference

- Contrary to popular belief, when you think of yourself as a collection of personalities with differing thoughts, feelings, and priorities, you will actually feel more sane.

- Check frequently on what kind of questions you are asking yourself. Is your committee asking good questions that will lead to positive outcomes?

6

Two:

Identifying the Should
Monster in Charge

Now that you are a crowded conference room rather than one single, individual reader, it's time to ask, "Who is in charge of this group I call me?"

For anyone seeking help to learn self-forgiveness, the answer to this question will probably be found in the all-too-familiar aspect of personality known as *self-criticism*. Hint: It's the big shot who does all the talking.

I often ask workshop participants, "How many of you consider yourselves to be particularly self-critical?" The responses vary greatly from audience to audience.

You might think that the prevalence of people who consider themselves to be self-critical would vary according to whether or not they are especially hard on themselves. That's what I thought at first; it seemed logical. But as I continued to give talks and facilitate workshops about self-compassion, I learned that the various responses to my question had more to do with people's level of self-awareness, and specifically to do with how they defined "self-critical."

It seemed that the more time I spent with participants, the more self-critical they became. Could I have been having such a negative effect on people who expected to be helped by what I had to say? Gratefully, I don't think that I was causing the negative effect.

High Tolerance

Just as alcoholics have a high tolerance for alcohol, people who are excessively self-critical have a high tolerance for their criticism and the feelings that it evokes. Alcoholics may not consider themselves drunk even after several drinks, and others will often not perceive them as drunk due to their increased tolerance. Having alcohol in their systems has been "normalized." We say that they can hold their liquor.

Similarly, even excessively self-critical people may not appear so outwardly, and because tolerating self-criticism is "normal" for them, they may not identify their self-criticism as a problem. With constant exposure to self-criticism, a tolerance is built. We could say that they can hold their self-criticism. They may even value their high tolerance to self-criticism as a strength.

> The excessively self-critical can withstand extreme
> amounts of personal attack, from self and others,
> without necessarily showing the effects outwardly.
> But make no mistake: Tolerance to pain or poison
> is not an attribute; it is part of the problem.

We tend to habituate to self-criticism just like we do to any particular sound in our environment that is constant—for instance, the steady hum of some appliance or machinery. That is, we unconsciously "tune out" the constant sound in order not to be distracted by it. When a visitor to the environment notices the buzz of my old refrigerator and asks me, "What is that sound?" I reply with my own question, "What sound?" In the same way, we may "tune out" self-criticism, but we are not able to easily escape the emotional, mental, and physical effects of the "constant buzzing within."

Others who are self-critical will be obvious to the outside world: It's like they have the external speakers turned on so that we can all listen to their unrelenting criticism and negativity about themselves. Frequently, these people are constantly apologizing, whether or not they have done anything wrong. (I'm sorry I said that.) The folks with their external speakers turned on still have the same high tolerance—sometimes an even higher tolerance—and therefore do not take effective action to change things for the better. They just keep criticizing and apologizing.

Still others will be stoic as they stand constantly in the line of self-critical fire, but will be detectable outwardly via persistent physical complaints, including headaches, body pain, and fatigue. Again, the tolerance remains high, particularly when there is little or no awareness of how the perpetual negativity is playing into the symptoms.

All of that can change.

A New Way of Thinking about Self-Criticism

The reason that audiences I spend more time with "become" more self-critical is that as I describe self-criticism in new terms to them, their self-awareness increases. They begin to find the hidden pictures, to experience self-criticism in terms of their inner relationship. They become not more critical, but more aware of the constant "noise" in their heads—the noise they had previously habituated to, or the "noise" they had previously accepted as their normal experience.

Here is a simple idea with great potential: You can have a relationship with your self-criticism rather than remaining in the powerless and exhausting position of being self-critical. And as you learn to think of this as a relationship, you'll begin to establish the ability, and eventually the power, to do something about it. You are opening the door to change; you are giving yourself the opportunity to disagree with a negative opinion.

The Should Monster Revealed

Meanwhile back in the conference room ... The big shot (big bully is more like it) who is usually in charge of the committee is a character I call the *Should Monster*.

I have been describing this much dreaded and ever present committee bully to audiences for years, and I have never had to explain at length who (or what) this Should Monster is. Audiences recognize it almost instantly.

The Should Monster is the inner critic that accompanies us inexhaustibly through our daily lives. The Should Monster believes that it knows best, offers advice freely, and is always available—and more than willing—to tell us what we *should* do or how we *should* be different in some way. To this constant inner critic we are never enough. We can never be enough and we can never do enough. The monster is never satisfied. And unless we can find a way to pry ourselves loose from the Should Monster and its predictably negative opinions, we will never be satisfied.

Your Should Monster won't show up with a name tag that says *Should Monster* or *Inner Critic* or *Bully* or *Your Personal Tyrant*. It will tell you that it is your best friend, your only hope. Mine used to say, "Thom, if it weren't for me lighting a fire under your butt, or hanging a carrot in front of your face, you would have accomplished nothing in your life. I'm here for your own good, and don't you forget it." I would respond obediently with the appropriate shame, having been "put in my place." There were times when I expected to hear my Should Monster tell me that it was "the Truth, the Light, and the Way." I suppose not saying it was my Should Monster's idea of being subtle.

Your Own Personal Monster

Every Should Monster is unique, with its own particular demeanor and style. Some are not as blatant as mine—mine never hesitated to jump up and down in my mind calling me names and threatening me. Some are much more subtle, even subliminal, but every bit as powerful. And when challenged, any Should Monster will become quite intimidating.

I frequently remind my clients to beware of the Should Monster that waits in the car, ready to talk to them on the way home from therapy sessions: "I can't believe you said that about your parents!" or "Don't you think that you were exaggerating things just a bit? There are people in the world with *real problems*, you know!" or "You are beyond hope. Don't you know that you are wasting your time talking to that silly man . . . *and paying him for it!*" I'm always amazed how—in one breath—the Should Monster will tell us that we are the worst of the lot *and* that there is nothing wrong with us.

These perpetual advice givers are especially fond of Monday-morning quarterbacking, offering a steady stream of *you should have thises* and *you should have thats*. Toss in a few *if onlys*, *what ifs*, and the always popular *you can never get anything right*, and there you have it: a well-rounded, highly effective Should Monster.

The best Should Monsters (as if it's a competition) are masters of the questions that are not questions: "Why can't you ever stick to a diet?" "What makes you think you could ever be in a healthy relationship?" "Why don't you just give up?" (or "Why do you always give up?")

Whatever the style, your own personal monster is probably the source of that pervasive guilt or shame you carry in your gut, chest, or head. It will *not* be the source of any genuine forgiveness. And it is probably in charge of your committee.

And remember: This tyranny is inwardly directed. Some people with the most ferocious Should Monsters are outwardly the kindest and gentlest of friends, employers, co-workers, and family members. We operate with a dangerous double standard that most simply states, "You deserve a break. I don't."

Decreasing Tolerance

Once self-criticism is translated into a relationship with your Should Monster, you may feel overwhelmed by the control that your monster has over your feelings, thoughts, and actions. Hang in there. As you become increasingly aware of how toxic this relationship is, you can be sure that your once high tolerance for self-condemnation is on the decline.

As your tolerance for the criticism decreases, it is only natural that you will feel worse. You will be in touch with the feelings that anyone would reasonably experience as the recipient of such unfair judgment. This is an opportunity for you to have empathy for yourself—which by the way has nothing to do with feeling sorry for yourself, contrary to your Should Monster's opinion.

And just as we depend on physical pain to draw our attention to injury or illness of the body, the emotional pain experienced when faced with the abuse from the Should Monster is also signaling, "This hurts. Something is wrong here. Do something." The pain and discomfort is going to become an essential ingredient in your new determination to change the dynamics of this long-standing, exhausting relationship.

A Healthy Split

We tend to identify—even to agree—with the negative opinions of our Should Monsters. These opinions are often expressed with such confidence, authority, and constancy that we automatically and without question accept them as fact. Brainwashed. Old habits die hard. And so on.

The relationship with your Should Monster is based on the codependent rule that whatever you think of me will determine how I will feel about myself. Can you identify relationships, in the past or present, that are (or were) based on this rule? These are relationships in which you have handed over your personal power to another person—a spouse, a parent, a child, a friend, and so on. The relationship with your Should Monster is based on the same principle, and blindly obeying this rule—in any relationship—can only lead to feelings of lowered self-worth, discouragement, and shame, none of which are of much help in learning to forgive yourself.

In order to intervene in this inner codependent relationship, it is necessary to learn to tell the difference between your Should Monster and yourself. By consciously shifting your identity from the messenger to the recipient of the messages, you will take a giant step toward creating a space for forgiveness. In essence you are placing the Should Monster outside of yourself, front and center, and you are listening to what it has to say. Afraid or not, you are not hiding. You're Gary Cooper and it's *High Noon*.

As you learn to distinguish yourself from your monster, it is not unusual to discover that you may agree with some or all of the negative, critical messages. Don't panic. I guarantee that if you continue to practice separating from your Should Monster and learn to identify yourself as *the recipient* of the shoulds, your responses will slowly but surely change. They will move toward a much healthier, empowered, and realistic position characterized by this statement: [You speaking to your Should Monster] "I see you. I hear you. I know who and what you are. And I disagree with you." And as you learn to disagree, shame will give way to anger, and that anger will become necessary fuel for making this healthy split. As Popeye the Sailor says, "I've stood all I can stands, and I can't stands no more!"

So, who is in charge of the committee? The answer is probably the Should Monster ... *for now*. Here's a suggestion: For the next five to seven days, practice the journal exercise that follows. Then reassess your relationship by rereading this chapter.

> Anger is not the problem; it is an
> important part of the solution.

Getting Better Acquainted with Your Monster

What's in a Name?

You may want to name your inner critic something other than the Should Monster. For me, Should Monster was the perfect name—I thought of it as my *should-er on my shoulder*. One of my clients calls her monster IT, with capital letters. Other names I have heard: the Warden, the Punisher, the A—hole, the Programmer, the Supervisor.

He, She, or It?

Trust your intuition when it comes to thinking of your Should Monster in terms of gender. Some men I have worked with have had a critical voice they clearly identified as female. And the large majority of the women I have talked with about their Should Monsters automatically refer to them as *he*.

Journal Exercise

Your Inner Relationship

The following exercise is a powerful way to practice distinguishing yourself from your Should Monster. Trust your intuition with this exercise; there is no wrong way to do it. If you think there is, it's likely that your Should Monster is trying to supervise your work. Give yourself room to explore, keeping in mind that the purpose is to increase awareness; it's not about pushing yourself to change. Remember to let the power of awareness (chapter 3) work for you.

Divide a page in your journal into two columns. Label one column "Should Monster," and for now, leave the second column blank. In the Should Monster column, start a list of some of your Should Monster messages. Some may be general criticisms that you live with constantly. Others may be insults and put-downs specific to certain situations or relationships in your life.

If you're thinking that this sounds negative (sort of anti-Norman Vincent Peale), you are absolutely correct. The messages of inner abuse are negative. But the increased awareness that will result from keeping track of your specific messages is positive. To the degree that these should messages remain hidden from conscious awareness, they will maintain a powerful, subliminal effect on you. Before a problem can be effectively solved, the nature of the problem must be clearly defined. And you must learn to walk toward the problem, even when the most natural reflex is to duck and cover. In fact, our Should Monsters are powerfully reinforced every time we submit to their intimidation.

Now here is the twist: Write each message to *yourself* in the second person, with your name preceding each message. In other words, write the messages *from* your Should Monster to you. For example, "Thom, you are a selfish, ugly person . . . Thom, you should work harder . . . Thom, you are lazy."

Notice the progression from specific to general in the following examples: Thom, you are doing a sloppy job writing this chapter [specific]. Thom, what made you think you could ever make it as a writer [more general and a rhetorical question]? Thom, you have no talent [even more general]. Thom, you don't deserve to breathe [that should cover it].

Continued on the next page.

Journal Exercise—Your Inner Relationship—*continued.*

Now write some of your should messages in your journal. Here are a few more examples:

Should Monster	
Thom, you are lazy and useless.	
Thom, what makes you think that you have anything worth sharing with others? Why don't you keep your stupid thoughts to yourself?	
Thom, you will always be depressed just like the rest of your family. Give it up, loser.	

Notice that the messages do not have to contain the word *should*—often it is implied. Some may be general criticisms (directed at who you are) and others will be more specific (directed at what you do or don't do). You may or may not be aware of a message's origin. Some people will instantly recognize the source of a message, as in, "This is exactly what my father/mother/brother/teacher used to say to me." Others will identify the should messages as only their own thoughts.

And listen for the should messages in the form of rhetorical questions that are not questions at all, but imply that you should be different: "Why do you always have to screw things up?" "How do you expect others to have a chance to speak if you don't shut up?" "Why are you the way you are?" The shoulds are implied, but they are not subtle.

List five to ten of your should messages. Then read them aloud to yourself two or three times, paying careful attention to your responses. Try reading them into a mirror to yourself. How do you feel emotionally? Describe your physical responses. Is there a knot in your stomach? Tightness in your chest? Do you feel numb, emotionally or physically? Stretch your awareness. Learn as much as you can about how you are responding to your should messages. Write this information in your journal.

Continued on the next page.

Journal Exercise—Your Inner Relationship—*continued.*

I have one client who calls this exercise "pronoun therapy," referring to the shift from first to second person when writing the should messages. And in fact, this simple pronoun substitution can become the beginning of a powerful ripple effect of change in your life.

There is a big difference between walking around thinking "I am worthless," or "I can never get it right," and being followed around by someone who is telling you, "You are worthless," or "You never get it right." You may not experience the difference immediately, but when you continue to practice the separation from your Should Monster with this "pronoun therapy," your tolerance for self-criticism will significantly decrease. Regardless of how low your self-esteem is, if someone were to follow you around day and night, insulting you and criticizing you at every turn, that someone would begin to get on your nerves.

By practicing this simple exercise, you are taking a stand—a stand of separateness from your Should Monster. This is a declaration of independence.

Responding to the Should Monster
When you are ready, use the blank second column in your journal to write your responses to the should messages. You can label this column "My Responses." For each message, write two responses: First, your thinking response—your opinion. In its simplest terms, this response is one of agreement or disagreement with the message. You may be in agreement with some (or even all) of your Should Monster's messages. I call this the "yes position," and it is frequently the first response as you begin to separate from the monster. At this point, having a different opinion is not as important as having a separate opinion.

The second response to write for each message is your emotional response. Once you hear the message and become aware of your opinion, what are you feeling? When you agree with the message, guilt or shame will be the predominant feelings. When you move toward disagreement, you will experience less shame and more anger. It's not unusual to feel numb, neutral, or "split off" in response to the criticisms; some people will reflexively abandon their own awareness, their senses, even their bodies (this is referred to as dissociation) and leave them to the Should Monster. It's a little bit

Continued on the next page.

Journal Exercise—Your Inner Relationship—*continued.*

like car-jacking, except instead of your car, it is your mind and body that are stolen.

Here are some examples of responses to the Should Monster:

Should Monster	My Responses
Thom, you are lazy and useless.	Opinion: I know it. Feeling: I feel awful—Shame.
Thom, what makes you think that you have anything worth sharing with others? Why don't you keep your stupid thoughts to yourself?	Opinion: Wait a minute. I have a good track record helping other people in therapy, in workshops, and with my writing. Feeling: Irritated, angry, defensive
Thom, you will always be depressed just like the rest of your family. Give it up, loser.	Opinion: I hope not. I don't want to believe that depression has to define my life. Feeling: Some strength. Lots of fear.

I call this the two-column exercise. Work with it for the next couple of days. If by then you are finding it to be helpful, continue the two-column journaling for the next week to ten days, remembering that the only objective of this exercise is to learn to distinguish yourself from your Should Monster.

Write a few should messages and your corresponding responses each day just for practice. Also, this is an excellent "emergency" exercise to use any time you are being barraged with self-criticism. Use the exercise to pry yourself away from the destructive grip of your Should Monster; with just a little bit of space between the two of you, you may be surprised how your responses will begin to change.

Points of Reference

- Self-criticism will not go away easily, but you can learn to disagree with negative beliefs about yourself.

- Make a daily practice of separating from your Should Monster. Remind yourself, "It is over there. I am right here."

7

Three:
Understanding the Should
Source

When you can understand where your self-criticism comes from, it will become much easier to develop an identity for yourself that is separate from your Should Monster. Understanding, however, is not an end in and of itself, but it does make the important work of letting go of negative thinking about yourself easier.

Should Monsters are not villainous by design. And they are not some sort of renegade personality fragments that have turned on us due to a freak mental mutation. In fact, Should Monsters tend to enter our lives for good reasons, and have very good intentions. Sometimes I think of them as well-meaning, but misguided, parents.

When your Should Monster says, "This is for your own good," it means it. It believes that it knows what's best for you. That, in and of itself, is not a problem. As you have discovered in the last two chapters, there's plenty of room in there for the committee's multiple opinions, even the not-so-helpful ones. The problem is the nearly impenetrable credibility the Should Monster can gain in your consciousness.

The Problem of Power

As you practice separating from your monster, as you translate self-criticism into the context of a relationship, you may feel overwhelmed with the amount of power that your Should Monster wields. One of my clients described it like this: "My Should Monster does more than intimidate me into submission and obedience. He possesses me. It is literally as if I stop existing and the Should Monster takes over."

This client is a perfectly sane, extremely successful woman in her late thirties. She is not given to explorations of the occult; she doesn't tend to exaggerate—and yet, she describes her relationship with her Should Monster as one of complete possession. Since hearing her description, I have discovered literally hundreds of people (clients and workshop participants) who identify with it.

Another client described her Should Monster relationship like this:

> It's an extremely abusive relationship, and I feel powerless to
> fight back, or to get away. It's like the classic "battered woman
> syndrome," in which the abused woman's self-esteem suffers to
> the point of believing that she deserves "what she gets," and that
> if she tries to escape, the abuser's fury will escalate and hurt her
> worse. I'm literally my Should Monster's hostage.

The client offering this description is a very busy, and highly effective, mother of three and part-time interior designer. She and her husband have been married for twelve years. At times she has complained of her husband's passivity, but she makes it clear that there is only one abuser in their home—her Should Monster.

Many others—men as well as women—have identified with this description of the trapped abuse victim or hostage.

Journal Exercise
Your Relationship with Your Should Monster

Write a description of your relationship with your Should Monster. If the relationship is more abusive at certain times or under particular circumstances, include that information in your characterization. For example, is your Should Monster more active or more harsh in a work setting, or in the area of personal relationships? I know one man whose Should Monster does not disturb him at all when he is at work, but in all other areas of his life, it is constantly on his back. As you might imagine, he is a workaholic.

Good Intentions

So how can something so bad, something so controlling, and something so arrogant possibly have good intentions?

Here is how I describe it in my workshops: Imagine that I'm giving a talk on the natural connection of self-forgiveness and personal responsibility. There is a well-dressed young man sitting in the second row, on the aisle. Every so often (there doesn't seem to be a set pattern) this young man gets out of his seat, walks up to me, and slaps me. (Sometimes absurd metaphors are more fun.) After about forty minutes, and four or five slaps, the young man moves again, this time simply shifting his position in his chair. But with the first sign of his movement, I reach up with my right hand and slap myself. Then I look at him and say, "Don't worry. I took care of it." I am, of course, protecting myself—hoping that my having already been slapped will reduce or extinguish the young man's need to slap me again.

This is an absurd explanation, but it demonstrates a couple of important points. First, the tolerance that the audience and I show for my being slapped by the young man represents the high tolerance we have (individually and community wide) for the unfair treatment of ourselves and others. Second, when I slap myself in this silly little story, I am acting as a Should Monster acts. That is, having learned that something painful is on its way, and *not* having learned that I have a choice in the matter, I take it upon myself to inflict the abuse before someone else can. The secret to this tactic is that I actually slap myself with a little less force than the young man has been using, thereby reducing the amount of pain I suffer. And I have created at least the illusion of control: I can decide when and how I get slapped.

Birth of a Monster

As children, we were learning sponges, absorbing the lessons around us without bias or preconceived notions. Filtering so little out, we learned to perceive our environment as it really was. And based on these innocent, but accurate, perceptions, we developed the defense mechanisms necessary to protect ourselves mentally, emotionally, or physically.

When, over extended periods of time, we experience mental, emotional, or physical "slaps," we respond by learning how to slap ourselves first. Enter the Should Monster.

A close friend of mine, Mary, tells this story:

I had my sixth birthday party at my grandmother's house. All of my friends were there, and I was very excited. When it was time to play Duck, Duck, Goose, I sprang forward, volunteering to be "it" first. From out of nowhere I was lifted—more like jerked—off the ground and taken aside by my grandmother. She quietly, but harshly, told me, "Always let your guests go first." My friends witnessed the whole thing, and I was crushed.

Looking back, I realize how much that incident affected me. For me, at six years old, this was not a lesson in manners. The message that got through to me was loud and clear: "How dare you try to step forward and be special! You have no right to be special, even if it is your birthday." At forty-three years old I am still aware of this message inside of me. And it is still difficult for me to allow myself to be treated as special, especially on occasions like birthdays.

When one incident appears to have such a powerful impact on a child, it usually indicates that the experience—and the messages that went with it—is representative of the child's general experience. Of course, Mary's Should Monster would probably have us believe that she is making a mountain out of a molehill.

As an adult, Mary finds herself in a double bind: she has a strong, unfulfilled need to be special, accompanied by a persistent feeling of shame for having the need. If she acts according to her need, volunteering to be "it," her Emily Post Should Monster jerks her up and reminds her, "You should always let your guests go first." Her Should Monster is essentially scolding her, putting her in her place, before the present day equivalent of her grandmother does. Her Should Monster is saying, "Don't trouble yourself. I have already humiliated Mary. I don't think we'll have any more problems out of her for a while."

Tracking the Should Source

And where do we learn all this? At home, of course. And in our schools and churches and temples. We live, after all, not just in dysfunctional families, but in an imperfect and often dysfunctional world. But for the majority of us, our families provide the most prevalent, most consistent (or at least constant), and most direct learning experiences. Examining these lessons learned at home, though necessary for understanding the power of our Should Monsters, can be treacherous.

Exploring our families as the source of our Should Monster problems presents a couple of potential pitfalls. To one extreme, we are in danger of blaming our families for all the problems that we face today. This can only lead to immobilizing beliefs of victimization—"I am only the sum of my experiences." To the other extreme, there is the danger of refusing to honestly look at our families' contribution to our problems, for fear of being disloyal or irresponsible for blaming them. Taking this position leads to another kind of victimization in which we take on all the blame ourselves; the Should Monster heaps it on, and we accept it. The resolution, not surprisingly, will be found at neither of these extremes, but somewhere in the middle range.

Journal Exercise

Tracking a Should Source

Are there incidents from your childhood that have had a lasting negative effect? If so, try writing about them from the perspective of that younger you.

Maybe you do not identify a particular incident, but are aware of a general pattern of interaction that had a similar effect. If so, write about that general pattern. For example, "Whenever I accomplished something, my Dad told me I could have done better."

Codependent Some More

During the 1980s a new and improved understanding of addictive disorders gave birth to the codependency movement. Largely, the results of this movement were extremely positive. More people than ever began to reach out for much-needed help. And getting that help became more acceptable—ultimately, it even became fashionable. However, there were side effects that were not so positive.

In the name of learning how to take care of ourselves, many of us (and I was right in the middle of it all) dug into an us-versus-them mentality. Our parents were seen as the perpetrators, and we were their unsuspecting victims. We were the good guys and they . . . weren't.

This is not to say that parents can't be perpetrators. I have treated, and continue to treat, many adult clients who were seriously harmed by their parents' actions, inactions, or both. The problem is, as usual, the trap of all-or-nothing thinking. Rather than seeing the concept of dysfunctional families along a continuum, too many of us simply jumped on the wagon with the most severely abused, claiming that where the abuse wasn't apparent, it was even more horrendous in its deceptiveness. And during those codependent '80s, you could always find a therapist to support your newfound victimization. It became big business.

The Middle Range

By the time I had completed the manuscript for my first book (*Simple Truth*, 1990), I had shifted directions and was exploring family-of-origin learning from that middle range. Most descriptions of codependency were looking less like pathology and more like excellent descriptions of the pitfalls of being human. To me, as well as to others at the time, it seemed essential that we be able to discover the influence our families have on our development without becoming distracted by labels or blame. (Most clients I've worked with are eager to *not* blame their parents, but reluctant to modify their self-blame. It is equally important to let go of both.)

Around that time, I began to think of families as schools, learning centers teaching each of us how to be in the world—how to survive and/or thrive. And lesson one is always "How to Define Myself."

Family Lessons

So, families are our alma maters, the schools we attended to learn how to be the people we are now. No matter how much we might like to think of ourselves as separate from the families from whom we first learned, any of us beyond adolescence have recognized our parents in our own actions, words, and thoughts. I once told my stepdaughters (in a loud, authoritarian voice) that "beds were not made to be jumped on."

As children, we were wide open, especially to our parents and other family members. Instinctively we wanted and needed to trust them. We faithfully recorded the messages—the family lessons—like a hungry blank tape. We recorded spoken and unspoken messages alike. The silent messages were especially powerful and easily remain hidden in our adult lives since we never actually heard anyone speak the message aloud.

Sometime between early childhood and adulthood (the timing seems to vary greatly) we re-recorded the family lessons in our own voice. Same script, new voice. My voice. And your voice.

And so when a client walks into my office, sits down, and begins to berate himself, frequently without awareness of the self-abuse, and I ask, "Who is telling you all of these mean things about yourself?" the answer usually comes back, "I am."

It is important that you become more consciously aware of *what* was taught, and *how* it was taught at your alma mater. But to do so, you don't have to judge your family as either functional or dysfunctional. With a commitment to remain open-minded and fully responsible for yourself, viewing your "family education" along a continuum will become not only possible, but it will also provide a much more productive approach to your family-of-origin exploration.

Pocket Questions

Try any or all of the exercises in this chapter. Share your experience with others. And the next time you experience conflict or discomfort in your life, reach into your pocket and pull out these questions:

- What did my alma mater teach me about this _____ ?
  (subject, situation, feeling, etc.)

- Who taught me about how to handle this?

- (And most importantly . . .) How do I choose to handle it today?

Once you've located your should source and the truth of your family curriculum is consciously known to you, you can go back to school—enroll in the University of Free Choice (UFC) where every applicant is accepted. Corny, but true.

Journal Exercise

Taking Inventory

There are a number of approaches for taking stock of family lessons. Most psychotherapies revolve around one approach or another for becoming aware of and/or changing these lessons or belief systems. Certainly, an accurate inventory of what we learned, did not learn, and mis-learned in our families-of-origin is central to the task of developing self-compassion.

For the remainder of this chapter, let go of either/or judgment about yourself and your family. Consider yourself not as a product of function or dysfunction, but a product of imperfect family lessons. What follows are three different approaches for taking inventory of your family lessons. Use what is helpful. Mix and match.

Who Taught What
Make a list of significant adult family members in your childhood. Include any adults who come to mind when you recall your family, whether or not they are blood relatives. These were your teachers, for better or worse, directly and indirectly. Review each name on your list one at a time. Close your eyes and visualize (or just think of) that person as he or she appeared to you when you were a child. In your mind, use the name for that person that you used as a child. Tuning into each of these relationships, write down what you learned from each person. Consider what you learned about yourself from how these people treated you. Consider also what you learned from how they treated themselves and other family members. What did you learn from what they said? What did you learn from what they did or did not do? Trust you intuition; forget about getting the "right" answers and just write whatever comes to mind.

What You Learned about What
Money. Spirituality. Feelings. Particular feelings like anger, guilt, shame. Happiness. Work. Being a man. Being a woman. Being a

Continued on the next page.

Journal Exercise—Your Inner Relationship—*continued.*

friend. Being a spouse. Deservingness. Giving. Receiving. Sex. Being a spouse. Being a parent. Being a son or daughter. Alcohol. Religion. Love. Communication. Family. Fun.

Consider these categories and whatever else springs to your mind. Consider areas of your life in which you experience confusion, rigidity, relationship conflict, or any other form of discomfort. List the categories of life issues that most concern you *now* in your adult life. Take each category from your list, hold it quietly in your mind for a minute or two. Then write down what your family curriculum taught about that particular subject.

For many of us, lessons about issues that are problematic today were either grossly mistaught or not taught at all in our families. Where we need wisdom, we discover erroneous beliefs or empty space. In either case, it can be helpful to recognize that the current dilemma is not due to inherent inadequacy or character flaws, but instead results from the less-than-accurate (or inadequate) education received from our alma mater families.

What You Decided When
There are certain times in our lives, perhaps certain life events, that precipitate psychological landmark decisions. These decisions greatly impact who we will become, what we will do, and how we will perceive ourselves in relation to the world around us. Sometimes these decisions are quite conscious. Sometimes not.

Draw a line—just a horizontal line across a sheet of paper with the left end of the line (marked zero) representing the beginning of your life and the opposite end being your present age.

Take a good look at your life in this overly simplified form. Mark on the line the age you were when you first left your family to live away from home. Look specifically at that space on the line between zero and your leaving-home age.

Tune into your conscious memory and your gut-level intuition. As you focus on this space on your time line, let your pen mark places (and indicate ages if you recall) when you made any milestone decisions. Don't worry about perfect recall; allow experimentation in your responses. Then write down the decisions you remember.

Continued on the next page.

Journal Exercise—Your Inner Relationship—*continued.*

Witnessing the dysfunction in a less-than-perfect family, many people will make life-affecting decisions at an early age, such as:

- Anger is violent. I must never be angry. Or I must never show my anger. Or Anger hurts people's feelings. I will never express my anger directly.

- I will never be like my father. Or I will be just like my father.

- It doesn't pay to be emotionally honest, so I'll tell people what they want to hear.

- Life is a no-win proposition, so I might as well give up.

- I won't let them keep me down. I'll succeed beyond all expectations and really show them.

- I'll be responsible for it all. If you want a job done right . . .

- I will never treat my kids (or my spouse) the way Dad/Mom treats me.

Points of Reference

- It is neither necessary, nor productive, to think of your family as all healthy or completely dysfunctional. Think, instead, in terms of what you learned there.

- Understanding how you became self-critical is an important part of self-forgiveness. The goal is to remove unfair blame from yourself, and it is not about finding others to blame instead.

8

Four:
Discovering the Decision
Maker

A client says to me: "Okay, I'll give you that. My so-called Should Monster has been running the show for as long as I can remember. But to tell you the truth, I'm not so sure that I'll be able to function *without* it. Crazy as this may sound, that unrelenting self-criticism has been the one constant in my life. And besides, what makes you think I can do a better job if and when I am in charge?"

I respond: "You probably will have difficulty once you separate from the monster. After all, you have been joined at the brain for all these years. By taking a stand now, you will be stepping into uncharted territory. Without your reliable old friend, who will you be? How will you get anything done? But I can tell you this: you *will* continue to function, even if you feel worse before you feel better. And as for what makes me think you can do a better job being in charge of your own life, I don't know that you can—at least not yet."

One thing that we may hate worse than being unforgiving of ourselves is being a beginner. Starting from scratch to learn something brand new—especially something we would like to think comes naturally—can be very frustrating. And there is always that strange comfort in sticking with the familiar, doing what we know, avoiding drastic change, no matter how painful or ineffective that may be.

A young man I had worked with for about a year came into his weekly session, took his usual seat, and wasted no time getting to work. "I think I've figured something out," he began.

> *We already know that I absolutely hate being a novice—at anything. And we know that I am a novice with a capital N when it comes to even giving myself the time of day. Nothing new there. Here's the piece I got after last week's session; it just sort of popped into my head when I was thinking about what you had said about my needing to be more than just competent at anything I do: Not only am I resisting the challenge of learning self-care from scratch, but I am also holding on to my "self-sacrifice" M.O. with a death grip because I am so good at it. I am way beyond competent at not taking care of myself, at putting everyone else's needs ahead of mine.*

That was an easy hour's work for me. This young man had taken a quantum leap into a simple, but potentially life-changing awareness: He had inadvertently learned to value being good at whatever he did over being happy. This is an excellent example of how personal value systems can get out of whack when we are not making conscious choices—when we are letting external circumstances and other people make decisions for us.

> The bad news is that I am relentlessly
> self-condemning; the other bad news is that
> I am very good at it.

Once we realize where the Should Monster came from and that it is not our friend, or at least is no longer working in our own best interest, what next? Stop criticizing ourselves, of course. Like the doctor says to the patient who complains, "Doctor, it hurts every time I do this": "Don't do that."

Well, Doc, if only it could be so easy. If only we could simply tell ourselves that we should not be so self-condemning, that we should not should on ourselves. The fact is, if that worked, you wouldn't need this book, and for that matter, there would have been no need for me to write it. But the Should Monster will usually step in at this point—having read every self-help book you have read, and having faithfully attended every one of your therapy sessions—to criticize you for being self-critical.

I used to tell my therapist that if there was an Olympic event in self-beratement, I knew I could win gold, because I could beat myself up for beating myself up for beating myself up.... Well, you get the picture. Maybe you think you have what it takes to take home a medal.

What You Need to Know about Changing

The Negative Command

One of the most important lessons to learn when it comes to any kind of conscious change process is to identify what does not work, and like the doctor said, *don't do it.* In mastering the ability to recognize what does not work, you increase the chances of achieving the change you desire and greatly improve your efficiency in getting there. Change is accomplished when you are able to divest energy from what is keeping you stuck, and reinvest that energy into more productive thought and action.

Most of us can do a pretty fair job of identifying what is not working for us. It's the next step, reinvesting the energy elsewhere, that usually trips us up: we try to stop doing what is ineffective by telling ourselves *not* to do it. For example, "Don't focus on the negative." "Quit thinking of all the various ways that you can fail." "Stop thinking about that person so much." "Don't focus on the delicious desert that you want." These are great ideas with positive intention, but this approach to change is doomed to fail.

In hypnosis, this is called the negative command and it works like this:

> *As you continue to read this book, as you are reading this very*
> *sentence, whatever else you do, whatever else you think,*
> *absolutely under no circumstances focus your attention on your*
> *left hand. Don't think about your left hand. Do not experience*
> *any sensations in your left hand. Certainly, don't allow your left*
> *hand to begin to feel in any way different or distinct from the*
> *rest of your left arm. Above all do not, I repeat, do not*
> *experience your left hand as having any kind of tingling feelings*
> *or sensations of lightness.*
>
> *Now, don't think of the color blue. Don't picture a purple*
> *elephant. And while you're not at it, don't see yourself at the*
> *bookstore buying two more copies of* The Self-Forgiveness
> Handbook *to give to friends.*

Demonstrating the negative command is one of my favorite things to do in workshops. I can see the initial struggle in people's faces as they try to obey the negative command, followed very quickly by the smile or laugh that accompanies the realization that compliance is impossible. Our brains simply will not compute the negative. In order to *not* do something, the brain has to access an image of the forbidden thought or action. So even when you are able to abstain from acting on a negative thought, you are still mentally rehearsing the negative.

Journal Exercise

Keeping Track of Those Negative Commands

Make a list of negative commands in your thinking. As you write your list, respect the positive intention behind each of them, while expanding your awareness of how and why these particular thoughts have been ineffective in promoting positive, lasting change in your life.

Pay attention to negative commands (yours and other people's) over the next few days and continue to add examples to your list. (In some ways, this may become an extension to your Should Monster messages.)

The Positive Command

Now, here is what I say in the second part of my workshop demonstration: Focus all of your attention on your right foot. Become completely aware of that foot, right there at the end of your right leg. Read slowly, pausing between sentences to increase your focus on your right foot. Move your right foot around and be aware of any sensations in that foot. Imagine that your right foot is becoming heavy, heavier than any other part of your body. A very heavy right foot.

Were you successful in remaining focused on your right foot? Did you think about your left hand? And if you did think about your left hand, were you still able to achieve a reasonable focus on your right foot? I'm willing to bet that you were certainly not able to ignore your right foot.

When I do this demonstration in workshops, some participants will report an experience of extreme focus on their right foot, while others—those who are always trying to stay a step ahead—will report at least some focus remaining with their left hand. Why? Because they are thinking that the right-foot exercise is intended to distract their focus from their left hand. Get it? They inadvertently give themselves a negative command: "Thom is guiding my attention to my right foot, away from my left hand. His purpose is for me to not focus on my left hand."

> I don't need anyone to get in my way; I can
> do it perfectly well myself, thank you.

Changing Focus

Since you can't should your shoulds away, since you have already proved again and again that this will not make you feel one bit better, and since the secret of avoiding the negative is focusing on the positive, what do you focus on now? Where and how do you reinvest your energy, especially with the Should Monster and his negative cronies taking up so much space (rent-free) between your ears? Often it is difficult to imagine that there is room for anything or anyone else.

A New Recruit

Return to your committee. Take a deep breath. Look in the corners of your conference room. Look under the conference table. Look in the hallway. Look for as long as you like. Then, walk over to a mirror on the wall and look directly at the image in the mirror. There it is. It may appear frightened or confused or helpless or chaotic or whatever, but this is your *Decision Maker*. (Say, "Hello.") Like it or not, this is the object of your new focus. It's time to take your rightful position: Chairman of the Board. Ready or not, your time has come.

Showdown

Imagine this: When your Should Monster speaks (or simply sends its vibe) you, the new recruit, stand in the line of fire. You don't step aside, you don't duck. You may flinch a little—after all, you're only human. Remember: you're Gary Cooper and it's *High Noon*.

The Should Monster speaks: "You are a lousy excuse for a (*fill in your own insult*)." You listen, unmoving. You consider the insult that has been fired your way. And then, taking a deep, cleansing breath, you return fire: "I disagree," you say. And then you turn and walk away.

For example, when the young man with the self-sacrifice M.O. steps into the boots of the Decision Maker, he will disagree with the belief that excelling in performance and impressing others is more important than his personal sense of well-being. More to the point, he will realize that

> The good news is that I have found my
> new recruit, the one who will become my
> Decision Maker. The bad news is it's me.

top performance and taking care of everyone else does not have to be his primary source of self-esteem.

The Power of Disagreement

Here is the best part: You don't have to outdraw, outthink, out-manipulate, outanything the Should Monster in order to claim your right-ful authority over your own life. To drain the Should Monster of *your* personal power, all you have to do is *disagree*. Again, this is easier said than done, but it is good news for everyone who has been trapped in a codependent relationship with their Should Monster. When you can rec-ognize the tremendous power of disagreement—without feeling a need to debate or convince—you can begin to let go of the need for the Should Monster to finally approve of you. The choice becomes clear: You can stay and wait for the Should Monster to finally let you off the hook, or you can create a mutiny of sorts, and take over, making your own deci-sions about how you will perceive yourself, and consequently, how you will feel about yourself. To remind me of this very important piece, I keep a little plaque on my desk that reads:

I reserve the right to disagree with myself.

Journal Exercise

I Disagree

Make a list of beliefs about yourself that you disagree with. Then make a list of beliefs about yourself that you want to disagree with. Now write a statement of intention to learn to disagree with your Should Monster. This is a declaration of independence written from the Decision Maker's perspective—your perspective.

Make a list of fears and objections that arise as you do this exercise.

Beginner

In order to develop a strong Decision Maker, you must be willing to be a beginner, to start from scratch to learn something brand new, to not be any good at it at first, to start over again and again. Ironically, this willingness to be so incompetent will become an important source of self-esteem. I frequently remind my clients that when we lay our heads down at night, it is often more important to feel good about ourselves than it is to just feel good.

Remember this Zen principle: The expert has nothing to learn, while the beginner (the novice with a capital N) has everything to learn. As a beginner, you can learn anything. You can learn how to focus on your right foot, or your left elbow. You can even learn how to use those negative commands ("Don't focus on your left hand") that you can't seem to shake as "springboards" to new, improved positive thoughts.

Springboard Thoughts

Try this: For the next couple of days, every time you even notice your left hand, use that awareness as a springboard to think about your right foot. In this way, the persistence of left-hand awareness ceases to be a problem, and actually becomes an aid to increasing your right-foot awareness.

As we walk around in our day-to-day lives, we tend to look forward, side to side, and down in order to find our way from here to there without stumbling over furniture or walking into walls. As navigators of physical space, our visual field does not usually need to include looking up. And so, without giving it any conscious thought, visually we will tend to be more aware of the middle to lower elements of our physical environment than we are of those that are higher. Put simply: Most of us know much more about the floors in our world than we do the ceilings. For the next couple of days, every time you become aware of a floor, instantly become curious about the corresponding ceiling. Again, one awareness—a well-ingrained, habitual pattern in this case—becomes the springboard to a new awareness. And so goes the work of a clever Decision Maker.

Enter The Decision Maker

My favorite scene in the original *Superman* movie, starring Christopher Reeve, is when we see Superman for the first time. Clark Kent has spent years of preparation in The Fortress of Solitude, and from a great distance we see Superman standing in the Fortress. And then the music builds quickly and briefly and Superman flies directly toward us, straight into the camera. The whole scene takes no more than fifteen seconds. For me this scene represents the emergence of power, the entrance of the Decision Maker.

Of course neither you nor I are Superman, but we are—we must be—the heroes of our own stories. The Decision Maker brings hope, and the knowledge and power to fulfill that hope. Rent the movie; check the scene out for yourself. And as Superman flies right toward you, imagine a big *D* on his chest instead of the *S*. The Decision Maker will become the fully responsible adult within—the one with the authority to forgive.

Experiment
Springboard Thoughts

Choose two or three old beliefs about yourself (you can take them from the previous journal exercise) that you would really like to change. Corresponding to each old belief, write a concise new positive belief that you would prefer. (You don't have to believe the new belief; you just need to want to believe it.)

Pick one of the old beliefs to work with for the next ten days. Memorize the new, positive belief that corresponds to that old belief. Every time you become aware of your thinking the old belief (left hand/floor), use that awareness as a cue to rehearse your brand new, preferred belief (right foot/ceiling). Mastering the springboard technique will take some practice, but it is well worth the effort—especially when you consider how wonderfully sneaky it is to actually use the negative thoughts to help you learn the positive ones.

Points of Reference

- It is useless to criticize yourself for being self-critical. A Decision Maker takes charge without being negative.

- A Decision Maker uses negativity to create positive, productive direction.

9

Five:
Building the Power

Quite naturally, doubts and fears persist. You might be thinking,

I've been living my life by default, according to hundreds, if not thousands, of "fine print" rules—policies and procedures handed down to me by family, teachers, society at large, and even by chance. Now that I can see this, I most certainly don't like it. But who am I to swim against the current? Even if I wanted to, am I strong enough?

The concept of a Decision Maker is intriguing, but how does it work? How does it work in the real world? How will I know what to do, and how will I fuel my Decision Maker? Can this mild-mannered, even submissive, underdog really make such a difference in my life?

It is unnatural to be without our personal power. You and I are designed to operate by *decision*, not *default*. Certainly we want to be open to the influence and guidance of others, but ultimately mental and emotional health is the product of independent thought, as in: I respect your opinion, I trust my judgment. From this position, you can keep your defenses down, remaining available to hear the thoughts, ideas, and opinions of others without giving up your right and responsibility to think for yourself. Unfortunately, after years of giving power away to the others in your life and the Should Monster in your mind, thinking for yourself may not be well received.

Initially, bucking the system—breaking the rules that constrict you—will seem like swimming against strong currents. Often people involved in self-exploration and the recovery of free choice in their lives will experience powerful messages from outside and from within; these messages (be they feelings of fear or shame, interference from your Should Monster, or other people's expressions of disapproval or confusion) all say one thing, in capital letters: CHANGE BACK.

This is the resistance you will meet, in one form or another, to taking charge of your life. These are the obstacles you must overcome in order to live a life of self-compassion. The obstacles are not who you are, they are not the truth and they do not even belong to you. They are the inadvertent legacies from your past, your parents' past, your grandparents' past, and so on.

The Importance of Second Thoughts

I heard a story several years ago that exemplifies living by default:

> At a family reunion while a meal was being prepared, a little girl asked her mother why she cuts the roast in half before putting it (both halves) in the oven to cook. The mother thought for a moment, then shrugged her shoulders and suggested that the little girl ask her grandmother. After all, that is where she learned to cut the roast in two before cooking it. But she didn't remember her mother ever explaining why she did this.
>
> The little girl did as suggested and asked her mother's mother the same question. Again, there was the same shrug. The grandmother suggested that they go together to ask her mother (the little girl's great grandmother) why the roast was cut in two. After all, it was her mother who taught her, although she could not recall her mother ever specifically saying anything about cutting the roast before cooking it.
>
> All three—the little girl, her mother, and her mother's mother—were now very curious and went to ask the great grandmother about the roast. The little girl's mother's mother's mother did not shrug or seem puzzled at all. She simply said, "I had to cut the roast into two pieces to cook them separately because my oven was too small for the whole roast."

The Decision Maker's job is to be curious, to not settle for cutting the roast in two "just because." The power for your newly recruited Decision Maker will be found in these *second thoughts*. You can waste a

> How many rules do you automatically obey
> without giving them a second thought?

tremendous amount of effort and energy trying to change or get rid of the well-rehearsed, reflexive thoughts that characterize the Should Monster, the Cynic, the Defeatist, and so on. You can waste your time hoping to change the people in your life who have grown used to you handing out your personal power like candy on Halloween. Or you can learn to identify these negative, self-defeating messages for what they are, and then ask yourself the all-important questions, "Does this make good sense to me?" and "What is my opinion?" These are the Decision Maker's Questions. And the power of these questions will grow with dedicated practice.

When you have second thoughts, be ready for your Should Monster to have *third* thoughts, volleying back like a tennis pro. As you begin to think for yourself, and especially when you begin choosing to think well of yourself, your old friend will be there, always ready to interrupt your new thinking.

Say something positive about yourself, and you may hear or feel an objection kick you from the inside. If so, your Should Monster is interrupting your positive thought, sticking its big, ugly should-foot in the aisle to trip you.

Changing in the Real World

It would be wonderful if the world around you and within you would always welcome your efforts to embrace self-forgiveness—and be equally

---

Journal Exercise

Interrupting Yourself, Part 1

Begin to write positive thoughts about yourself—each thought can be different or you can repeat the same thought or thoughts. As soon as you become aware of a negative thought interrupting or objecting to what you are writing, change to a different color ink, and write the objection. Return to the positive thought until you are interrupted again, exchange pens and again write the objection. Continue with this for as long as you feel like you are learning something valuable, or until you have obtained a sense of the rhythm of your conscious positive thoughts and the automatic interruptions of negativity.

forgiving—but to expect immediate understanding and support is one more way to give away your power. When you begin with an expectation that your changes will be recognized as positive growth and celebrated as such, you are once again in danger of being dependent on the approval of others for your basic sense of self-esteem. I'm not saying that there will not be people in your life who will support and celebrate your growth, but instead that many of us have a strong tendency to look for approval where we are least likely to get it.

The Decision Maker's job in this case is to identify any tendencies to look for approval in the wrong places, and then redirect that energy toward accepting the reality of the situation (for example, if you have identified a brick wall, stop trying to walk through it), and finding the needed approval and support from sources who have it to give—with no strings attached. In this way, the Decision Maker builds credibility (and therefore, power) by working to avoid the pitfalls associated with your old, cyclical patterns, and leading the way to meeting the legitimate need for positive reinforcement. In other words, the Decision Maker works to intervene on previously ineffective and hurtful patterns of thought and behavior, and then decides what to think, and what to do instead.

All the while, an effective Decision Maker has no interest in destroying the obstacles encountered; the object is simply to navigate through the obstacles. This is analogous to learning your way around in a new city. To try to drive everywhere as the crow flies will be impossible because of all of the structures between you and your destination. In the real world you know that you must stick to the roadways if you intend to reach your destination.

Obstacles

In general terms, here are some of the obstacles (or objections) you might encounter when you dare to decide for yourself what you will believe:

- You might be wrong.
- You probably are wrong.
- You are always wrong.
- You'll be sorry.
- You are so ungrateful.
- You are so selfish.
- You will end up all alone.
- You will hurt others (and then they will hurt you.)

These messages may come from within your own consciousness (I have a client who told me that she had a Threat Monster every bit as powerful as the Should Monster.); they may come from family, friends, or co-workers; they may come in the form of verbal responses to or about you; or they may take the form of subtle (or blatant) behaviors intended to send the change-back message. Just think about how powerful a well-timed sigh can be.

It's unfortunate how often negative opinions (especially about ourselves) are automatically considered more credible than positive opinions. This is reminiscent of the line attributed to Groucho Marx, among others: "I wouldn't want to be a member of any club that would have me as a member."

It's Not the Thought That Counts

Consider your thoughts to be suggestions, or even recommendations (from the faithful committee), about how to perceive yourself, your surroundings, a particular circumstance or relationship, or whatever. To experience yourself as separate from your thoughts might initially sound a little strange, but to do so is to be a Decision Maker in a position of (at least) potential power.

Journal Exercise

Interrupting Yourself, Part 2

Let's try turning things around: This time begin writing negative thoughts about yourself, and when you feel an interruption to the negative, change colors of ink, and write the positive objection. Return to writing the negatives until the next positive objection, and continue as you did in the first part of this exercise.

A word of caution: You may fear that once you start with the negative thoughts about yourself, there will never be an interruption—that you will be lost in an endless barrage of self-criticism. The fear is understandable, but when you pay close attention to your inner dialogue, there will be some objection. The purpose of this exercise is not to create positive objections (they already exist), but to guide you to hear them and to give them credibility.

Continue to practice this exercise from time to time. Part 1 is an excellent way to identify objections (or obstacles) that stand in the way of your positive progress, and Part 2, when practiced regularly, will build your power to stand up to the school-yard bully within.

> It's not so much the thought that counts as
> your relationship to the thought.

From this more independent position, you have the right and the responsibility to choose (and use) the thoughts that you believe will work most effectively in getting the results you want. This is living by decision rather than default.

> The right to be in charge of your own life is
> always accompanied by responsibility.

You have already experienced (via the negative command exercise in chapter 8) that you cannot directly expel any thoughts. The good news is that it is not necessary. As you grow increasingly aware of the thinking that promotes discomfort, dissatisfaction, and pain in the name of protecting you from risk; and as you respond by creating new alternatives to the old, habitual thoughts, and as you practice being separate from your thoughts, deciding to put new, self-respectful, and self-forgiving thoughts into play, the balance of power will shift. It will take time and plenty of dedicated practice (as you'll read about in chapters 10 and 11), but I promise that when you remain committed to this work, you will regain your personal power. To possess your personal power does not mean that you will control everything within and around you, but it does mean that come what may, you will be in charge.

Power Redefined

Now there exists, right alongside of your old faithful Should Monster, a Decision Maker, a part of yourself that understands the difference between being in control and being in charge, and the difference between unnecessary self-criticism and proactive decision making. Among the Decision Maker's first duties is the redefinition of three important terms that have

> To an old, ineffective, pain-producing thought, you
> say: "I recognize you; I know who you are; I hear
> what you are saying . . . and I *disagree* with you."

previously been booby-trapped by the Should Monster. The terms are *need*, *strength*, and *power*.

Need

Admittedly, *need* is a four-letter word, but it is not a dirty word, a horrible insult, or indication of a great lack of character. In my workshops I ask, "How many of you have thought of yourself as 'needy' and considered it a deep-seated, even shameful, weakness?" In fact, far too many people have been repeatedly told by others that they are *too needy*. Others receive the message loud and clear nonverbally. The result is partial or complete shutdown of awareness of needs—natural human needs.

> When you lose contact with your needs,
> they do not cease to exist. They wait.

The Decision Maker represents a new and different perspective: being in touch with your needs is an essential component in becoming emotionally independent and responsible. An emotionally healthy person is one who is aware of needs and who is highly resourceful in getting those needs met. In this way the Decision Maker acts as the healthy inner parent for that needy (remember, it's not a dirty word) inner child we hear so much about.

Strength

A second term that will need some work is *strength*. When needy is thought to be a character flaw, strength is defined as *not needing*, as in, "If I don't have needs, then I won't be vulnerable." From this perspective, the idea that emotional vulnerability and strength can coexist is quite foreign.

A strong Decision Maker not only makes this coexistence possible; it makes a powerful partnership between vulnerability (tuning in to needs) and strength (resourcefulness in meeting those needs).

> To be the Decision Maker in your own
> life is to be open to the influence of others,
> and yet never controlled by it.

Power

Power must be redefined from something that is *wielded over another* to something that *emanates from within*. The power of the Decision Maker is not used to harm or take anything away from another. True power makes it possible to be in the world without disguise (arising from shame) or excessive defense (arising from fear).

A Powerful Decision

Self-forgiveness is a decision—a decision to no longer hold yourself accountable to impossible, perfectionistic standards, a decision to remember that you are involved in a lifelong education in which mistakes are not only permissible, but actually necessary to the learning process. And self-forgiveness is a decision to have faith in your own value system, to trust in your own essential—and imperfect—goodness. Needs and all.

> Perfectionism is a state of perpetual victimization.
> Decision making is a state of constant learning.

Experiment
Undercover T-shirt

This is an assignment that a friend and colleague of mine has given to her clients from time to time: When clients are having a difficult time "holding on to their power" in the face of stressful circumstances, my friend suggests they give a little time to creating a design and/or slogan they can draw or write on a T-shirt that can be worn beneath their clothing so that only they know about the special undergarment.

One client brought a blank white T-shirt to a therapy session, and together my friend and she designed a shield. On the shield were depictions of things and ideas that symbolized her personal power, including phrases like, "I'll choose my own opinions," "Step back," "I trust the person beneath the shield," "Anti-should shield," and a drawing of herself as a strong, powerful decision-making adult protecting a small child.

My friend's client wore her "shield" beneath a favorite sweater to a Christmas family reunion. She reported excellent results.

Try this arts and crafts approach sometime when you can use a strong tangible reminder of your right and your responsibility to take good care of yourself. You can create your power T-shirt alone, but I think that it is particularly empowering to have a supportive friend or therapist work with you; somehow the T-shirt is more powerful when someone else knows your secret.

This is a little embarrassing to admit, but sometimes when I'm especially nervous about a presentation I'm giving, I will secretly wear a T-shirt with the Superman emblem on it. It's kind of fun really.

Points of Reference

- Of yourself and other around you, ask plent of questions and listen attentively to the answers.

- This is no time to be polite. When you become aware of inner negativity, interrupt yourself immediately.

10

Six:

Learning to Succeed

Have you ever thought that you might not be successful accomplishing—or even setting—your goals because you are out of practice? Consider your family lessons as you did in chapter 7; maybe no one ever taught you how to succeed. Maybe you learned how to "get by" or how to "survive," but you never really learned the finer points of how to succeed.

Maybe you have become too accepting of your dissatisfaction. Maybe you have a really bad habit of thinking negative things about yourself. Maybe you keep listening obediently to what the Should Monster tells you because you didn't know you had a choice.

Maybe all of that can change.

Expectations

Ask yourself this: "In terms of my efforts to develop self-forgiveness, what do I honestly expect is possible?" Can you envision yourself as a self-forgiving, compassionate person, accepting full responsibility for taking excellent care of yourself? This is an extremely important question. Reread it, and write some of your immediate responses in your journal.

Too often, we keep plugging away at our efforts to change, based on other people's expectations—our family's, our spouse's, or even our therapist's. While other people certainly come in handy when it comes to building and maintaining a quality support system (more on this in chapter 11), the only expectations that really count are our own.

Journal Exercise

Going Before the Committee

Put these two questions to your committee, and listen carefully to *all* of the responses. What do *you expect* is possible? What do *you believe* you are capable of accomplishing?

Write responses from the points of view of three or four different committee members. Put yourself purely in one viewpoint, and then another. Remember to use the power of awareness—you are gathering important information.

Faced with these questions, many of us discover that we have very *low expectations* of what we believe is actually possible. The expectations are low because we have so little faith in ourselves. We have not been taught to think of ourselves as successful. Instead, we are programmed to look for flaws and to focus on them—like pouring salt in an open wound.

Often, we actually expect failure. Even when improvement is evident, the assumption is that progress is temporary and will soon pass. We are waiting for the other shoe to fall, for the rug to be pulled from beneath us. Again I ask, *What are your genuine expectations of you?*

What Are the Risks?

Allowing yourself to fully experience your dissatisfactions is a risk. Identifying what you want is an even bigger risk. Maybe the biggest risk is believing that you can have what you want, that you deserve it, and that you are capable of doing whatever it will take to manifest your dream.

What do you actually risk if you decide to believe in yourself? The answer is simple: You risk failing to live up to your expectations. If you have grown up surrounded by criticism—shoulds, oughts, if onlys—falling short of your expectations can be a painful experience. If you were not taught to value yourself for who you are, beyond what you do or don't do, when you fall short of a goal, you and your failure are synonymous. You don't just fail—you are a failure. Whereas someone accustomed to a nurturing, supportive environment will experience disappointment and frustration, you will be devastated. No wonder you avoid the risk of positive expectations. Within a negative belief system, positive expectations are nothing more than bait in a trap.

The self-saboteur's motto:
You cannot lose what you do not have.

Big Challenge, Bigger Challenge

Let's say you've thought it over carefully and decided to accept all the risks involved in expecting yourself to succeed. You're ready—self-forgiveness waiting in the wings—to do whatever it takes to set your sights and accomplish your goal. As each of your fears shows up (and you can bet they will) and states its case (threats like "If you do this, you'll be sorry"), you square your shoulders, raise your head, look right at the threat, and say, "I am willing to take the risk."

Success is much more a matter
of courage than of ability.

The conversation might go like this:

The Threat: If you do this, you will only be making a fool of yourself.

The Response: I'm willing to risk it.

The Threat: If you do this, you are going to make someone very mad.

The Response: I'm willing to risk it.

The Threat: If you do this, you are going to hurt someone's feelings.

The Response: (deep breath) I'm willing to risk it.

Now, here comes the tough part, the part that many will say is the greatest challenge: learning to *acknowledge, reinforce,* and even *celebrate* your progress. To meet this challenge, you may have to change your beliefs about yourselves 180 degrees. No small matter.

Journal Exercise

Taking a Risk

Make a list of the fears and threats you are likely to encounter when you take the risk of expecting success from yourself. Leave some space to add to your list as you become more aware of the threats.

A Lesson in Success (Stepping Up)

Imagine yourself at the bottom of a flight of stairs. There are a dozen steps to the first landing. Now consider how much progress you would make toward the first landing if you would only be satisfied getting there in one step. Even if you stretch your stride and make it to the fifth step with one giant step, you don't recognize the progress because you haven't made it all the way, so you step back to the beginning to try again. Even with a running start, you make it only to step seven. Back to the bottom step you go, defining yourself as a failure. Eventually, you give up, accepting that you are not even capable of making it to the first landing.

Are you willing to do whatever it takes
to succeed, even if that includes the radical
idea of thinking well of yourself?

This scenario sounds ridiculous, but it accurately describes how you may be sabotaging your own efforts by defining success in all-or-nothing terms.

By imagining the flight of a dozen steps, you can easily see how to get to the first landing, and it is obvious that you could just as easily make it to the next landing using this amazing technique: *taking* one step at a time.

This very same amazing technique is how you can learn to succeed. The idea is to build a large success out of many smaller successes. Your challenge, and your responsibility, is to become supportive of your own efforts, to learn to recognize progress as it is happening (one or two steps at a time). Give yourself credit, and then get ready to take the next step.

But ... what if you are halfway to the first landing and you fall, tumbling back down to the bottom? The principle remains the same.

> Ultimately, it is persistence that pays off.

Taking one step at a time is still your best bet. Feel your frustration, express it—scream, holler, stomp your feet. Recognize the futility and the waste of energy of self-condemnation. Forgive yourself the misstep because it is the most energy efficient, productive thing to do; then start again.

Forget Perfection

It is doubtful that anyone who is reading (or writing) this book is not, to one degree or another, a perfectionist. Being a perfectionist does not mean that you do things perfectly; it means that you think that you are *supposed* to do things perfectly, that you are never satisfied with your efforts, that nothing you do is ever good enough. Advanced perfectionism manifests itself in the form of a person who has stopped trying to succeed. This person doesn't even make the effort because they are paralyzed by the fear of—and the expectation of—failure. And remember, this person's definition of failure is expansive, while their definition of success is very narrow, not to mention beyond human capacity.

One very important aspect of practicing self-forgiveness is reminding yourself that *perfection is not one of your options*. Perfection is not possible for us imperfect human beings, and striving for the impossible does not make us stronger; it tears us down.

> You can do great things and
> never come close to perfection.

Success Redefined

The most practical definition for self-forgiveness is *reasonable self-expectation*. With reasonable expectations, you are not automatically set up to feel badly about yourself. With reasonable expectations, you are given a chance to come out on top. With reasonable expectations, your latest accomplishment does not immediately become your minimal expectation. Where is the payoff in that?

The bottom line is, as long as the Should Monster and its cronies are defining success for you, you remain in a hopeless double bind: almost everything you think and do will be deemed a failure in one way or another, and in the event that a success slips through, that success will be used against you tomorrow. ("You are so inconsistent," your Should

Monster will say. "You blew it. You did fine yesterday, but leave it to you to drop the ball.")

Just as we redefined *need*, *power* and *strength* in the previous chapter, we must redefine *success* so that it can work *for* us, rather than against us. To define success in reasonable terms, we need to explore a couple of very important concepts: *goal setting* and *the confrontation of the obstacles* that stand in our way.

Goal Setting

In its simplest terms, goal setting is about getting from point A to point B. We are seldom at a loss to describe point A, the place of our dissatisfaction. But what do we know about point B?

Be Specific

If I tell you that I live in a little yellow house, could you find me? How about if I tell you that I live in a little yellow house on a corner lot across from a city park where a grammar school once stood? Well, that certainly is more information, and in fact, someone familiar with this city may very well be able to find my house with that information. But most people will need even more detailed information, like a street name and address, not to mention the name of the city. You are not likely to find the house if you just set out to visit, knowing that I live in a little yellow house on a corner lot. And yet, that is exactly what you are attempting when you seek change without setting specific goals.

A Simple Three-Step Plan

When you want to make a change, try this:

1. Describe in detail where you are now—the condition you want to change. (point A)

2. Describe in detail your desired destination—the change you intend to make. (point B)

3. Then, and only then, begin to identify the obstacles you are likely to encounter as you travel from point A to point B.

Consider how often you or others you know have approached a desire to change by focusing on steps 1 and 3 of this plan, but neglected step 2. When you remain focused on step 1, the result is inertia, and when you tend to focus on step 3 without having completed step 2, the predictable result is discouragement, or even a sense of hopelessness.

Applying the Three-Step Plan

Consider the following example: Sam is a client who showed up in therapy at the suggestion of a couple of friends. He was thirty-three years old when we first met.

When I look back at some initial notes from that first meeting, I notice that I jotted down four words as he talked about himself, the friends who had referred him, and why he might be wanting therapy. These are the four words: intelligent, creative, funny, aimless.

Sam didn't even seem all that unhappy. But his friends had grown weary of his increasing irritability, and he agreed that he had been "on edge" lately. One friend in particular, a woman Sam had known since college, was especially concerned. It had been a conversation with her that had finally convinced him to make the appointment with me.

The more Sam talked, the more aimless he appeared to me. Eventually he said, "My life is not turning out at all like I expected. I don't want to sound ungrateful, and maybe that's just life, but it feels kind of shitty to me." Sam had identified a starting point for our work together.

Step 1. To begin, I asked Sam to talk more about how he felt that his life was "not turning out at all like [he] expected." He responded first, as most people will, with feelings of guilt, returning to the idea that by expressing dissatisfaction he was being ungrateful, or that he was "just complaining." I explained to Sam that we are very capable of experiencing gratitude and dissatisfaction simultaneously, and that both are equally important. Dissatisfaction is like gasoline, I told him. If it is used correctly, it is fuel to take us where we decide to go. But if we just sit in it, breathing it in, it becomes quite destructive. I encouraged Sam to use his experience of dissatisfaction to his advantage, as fuel.

Don't waste your dissatisfaction. Use it!

Sam described a feeling of what he called "incompleteness," characterized by alternating periods of confusion ("still not knowing what I want to be when I grow up"); excessive self-criticism (Should Monster on the attack); and intense discouragement, at times bordering on a sense of hopelessness. Threaded throughout his "incompleteness" were times when Sam felt pretty good. He enjoyed his work as an advertising copywriter and had a lot of good friends—some of whom had suggested therapy.

My challenge with Sam—and the primary challenge of step 1—was to teach him to take his dissatisfaction seriously, to listen to it carefully, rather than trying to hide from it, or cover it up with activities or a heaping helping of Should Monster shame. It is the voice of dissatisfaction that ignites any process of change. Remember Popeye: "I've stood all I can stands, and I can't stands no more." With those immortal words, he would down a can of spinach and turn everything to his advantage.

Journal Exercise

Step 1

In what ways are you *not* taking your dissatisfactions seriously? How do they speak to you? How do you ignore them or postpone attending to them?

Listen very carefully to at least one dissatisfaction; then, from the point of view of the dissatisfaction, sit right down and write yourself a letter.

Step 2. As it turned out—as it often turns out—Sam had compromised himself more than he was able to comfortably tolerate. He rationalized that he was happy to be working in a creative field, but when he really began to explore that "happiness," Sam uncovered a lifelong dream that had been waiting patiently, fully intact, beneath the rationalizations, self-criticisms, and distractions. He was embarrassed, and a little afraid, to say it aloud; he told me that once he said it aloud, especially to someone who would very likely take him seriously, he was afraid that he could never take it back. And I happily told him that I hoped for that very dilemma.

Since he was fourteen years old, Sam had planned on being a novelist. That was the dream that had been buried. When he told me, I remember picturing it as a beautiful, old trunk full of buried treasure— buried treasure that Sam had unearthed.

Over the next few weeks, I guided Sam to explore and describe the particulars of his dream. What were the most important aspect of the dream? (I didn't want to assume about such an important matter.) Was it fame and/or fortune as a successful novelist that attracted him? Did he crave the experience of completing a novel? Or was he more inclined to lose himself in the creative process of writing? I asked many questions, and Sam learned how to formulate questions to help himself get closer to his dream.

Ultimately, Sam discovered that while he certainly aspired toward financial success with his writing, the more important aspect of the dream for him was the writing itself. At one point Sam said, "On the day that I die I cannot imagine regretting not having a best-seller. But I can easily see myself with deep regrets for not having made the effort." And that was that: Sam didn't need to make any drastic changes in his life. He remained in the same job, and even reported enjoying himself at work more—and feeling more creative. His friends were still his friends, *and* Sam spent a few hours each week writing. He didn't even begin with a novel. Instead, he started with short stories, and some poetry. Sam told me, "Since I can work the stories and the poems to completion in a relatively short time, they are helping to build my confidence. The novel is still in me, but that isn't what is most important. The main thing is that I'm writing for myself again."

By giving himself permission to openly explore his neglected dream, Sam was able to define (and describe) his desired destination in detail. In this way, a specific and relevant goal is established—otherwise known as point B.

Journal Exercise

Step 2

Describe a resolution for the dissatisfaction that wrote you the letter. Use a fair amount of detail in your description; and beware of any tendency to drift back to describing the problem. Write only what the *solution* will look like.

Step 3. Usually the trip from point A to point B is not as simple as knocking back a can of spinach. Once we know where we are, and where we want to go, there is still work to be done: navigating through the obstacles that lie between. Sam's situation provides a good example of the need to confront both external and internal obstacles.

External obstacles are those practical, real-life circumstances that we all face as we pursue our goals. For Sam, the primary external obstacles were regular commitments of his time that left little time to devote to writing. At first, as is often the case, Sam had difficulty seeing how he could make the time to write. Eventually, it became a matter of establishing his priorities, which resulted in his discontinuing his participation on a local board of directors and reducing the amount of time he spent playing racquetball in the mornings before work. He decided not to change his commitment to coach a little league baseball team and was able to hold onto Sundays as a "day off from everything."

The internal obstacles are often a little tougher to deal with. The major internal culprit for Sam turned out to be twofold: he fairly easily identified a lack of confidence in the form of a belief that he wouldn't be able to see his independent writing projects to completion, but he was surprised to discover that a little deeper down he felt as though he didn't deserve the "luxury" of doing what he wanted to do.

This problem of deservingness guided Sam's therapy toward some childhood experiences that seemed to at least confirm his erroneous belief, and may have had a hand in creating it. During that time, neither Sam nor I forgot that no matter what additional benefits the therapy might have—increased personal insight, improved family relationships, what-ever—our sights were set on getting Sam to write.

Journal Exercise

Step 3

Take an inventory of the potential obstacles between you and the goal you described in the previous exercise. Categorize the obstacles as (1) certain to be encountered, (2) possible to be encountered, and (3) not likely, but possible, to be encountered. (It is interesting to note how much valuable time and energy we sometimes spend worrying about potential obstacles that we may never encounter.)

More Lessons in Success (Breaking Through)

A couple of years ago, a colleague and I outlined a book we planned to call *Getting Unstuck: Overcoming the Obstacles That Keep You from Your Dreams*. The book never was written, except in the form of two or three magazine articles, but one of the "leftovers" from *Getting Unstuck* that I've always liked is the following combination guided imagery/poem that we wrote for the book:

The Wall

1

Imagine yourself standing in front of
a big, brick wall. Just you and the wall.
How close do you stand? And what
do you feel when you're facing the wall?
How wide is the wall? And how high?
Can you see the ends of the wall?
Can you reach the top?
How old is the wall—or how new?
Who built it—and why? How long
have you been here? Are you alone?
How long do you plan to stay?

2

It's your wall, you know. Touch it.
Feel its texture. Feel whatever you feel.
What is on the other side of the wall?
Can you guess? Do you know?

Have you ever been there?
Do you want to go there now?

3

What if you weren't alone? What if
there was more to this than
just you and the wall?
What if we were all there with you?
What if you were wrong
about the strength of the wall?
What if you were wrong
about your own potential?
You've been wrong before,
haven't you?

4

Your wall is made of bricks—
individual bricks.
The wall is big.
The bricks are small.
The mortar is of your own making.
How strong is it?

5

What if you regret
destroying your wall? What if
you miss it? What if you
can't handle it—on the other side
of the wall?
What if it's too late
to turn back now?

6

Now
when you touch your wall,
what happens? Push.
What happens? Both hands.
What happens?
How will you step through?
Do you dare? Can you
keep yourself from it?
Can you let yourself stumble,
and laugh—when you fall
through to the other side of . . .
What's left of the wall?

7

What is it like—on this side
of the wall? The sky, the ground,

the air around you—what is it like?
What do you see? What do you hear?
And how do you feel?
And what's that in the distance?

Try the imagery yourself. Have someone read the poem slowly and deliberately to you. Or record yourself saying it and play the tape back. Close your eyes as you listen, allowing the images to form. Kick the Should Monster out of the room for a few minutes; there is no wrong way to do this. Just listen to the poem, seeing whatever you see, thinking whatever you think, and feeling whatever you feel. Take your time. When you are finished, describe your experience in your journal. It can be interesting to return to this guided imagery in a few weeks, or even a few days. Write about your second experience and then compare the two.

This guided meditation/poem is not only about confronting the obstacles (the individual bricks that make up the wall) that stand between where you are and where you want to be, but also about how you might feel as you succeed in breaking through. It is not unusual to balk at the brink of success, especially when to do so requires plowing right through longtime negative beliefs about yourself. If you have been brought up to believe in the equation of *love equals sacrifice*, then you will surely feel guilt as you risk acting on the new belief of *I deserve to feel good about myself*.

The poem says, "What if it's too late to turn back now?" And, in fact, in the search for peace of mind, we will all eventually pass a point of no return, a time when we realize that we couldn't turn back even if we wanted to. And at that point, we do plow ahead, acting on shaky new beliefs about ourselves, and we do feel guilt in response. My wife, who is also a therapist, calls this experience *positive guilt*. I have heard her explain it in a lecture like this:

> *You will experience positive guilt when you are breaking the old,*
> *dysfunctional rules of your childhood. The guilt is like an addict's*
> *withdrawal symptoms: it screams for you to turn back, to get*
> *"back in line," to obey the old [often unspoken] law of the Should*
> *Monster, to "do as you are told." The guilt tells you that you are*
> *wrong.*
>
> *What makes it positive? Certainly not how it feels. The guilt*
> *is positive just as the addict's withdrawal symptoms are positive:*
> *it proves that change is underway. And positive guilt, like the*
> *addict's withdrawal, is pain for the purpose of clearing your system*
> *of what is toxic to you, so that you can start "clean."*

In the Distance

My favorite line in the poem is the very last one: "And what's that in the distance?" I can't know what you see in the distance, but for me it's like this: Having worked long and hard to break through the *Wall*, having stumbled across to the other side, I pick myself up, brush myself off, and look into the distance. What do I see? Another wall, of course. But before I rush to tackle the next wall, the more immediate challenge is taking the time to savor the success of breaking through this one.

Points of Reference

- Success involves taking one risk after another—risks that are based on your determination to take excellent care of yourself.

- You must not be blind to obstacles in your path, but be careful not to mistake them for your point of focus.

- When you have a success (small, medium, or large), admit it!

11

Seven:
Practicing, Practicing,
Practicing

At my house, I wash the dishes. My father before me washed dishes. And his father ... well, actually I don't think he ever lifted a finger in the kitchen.

When I have finished washing dishes, I know that I am not really finished. Within a very short amount of time—sometimes seconds—more dishes will begin to accumulate for me to wash. Occasionally this frustrates me, but I am never surprised by it. As long as my family and I live in a home of our own there will be dishes to wash. I expect it. I am not troubled by the ongoing, open-ended nature of washing dishes.

Establishing a daily practice of self-forgiveness is very much the same as washing dishes. For as long as we live in the world, there will be more to do.

There is an important choice to be made: we can perceive the ongoing nature of this work as endless and exhausting, and allow it to wear us down. Or we can choose to perceive it as our daily responsibility, and simply do it. To think of it as endless implies an expectation that there should be an end to it, that we should be able to finish once and for all. And to think this way is to set ourselves up for constant frustration and disappointment—to say the least.

Instead choose to live according to the old adage—that I have revised slightly—*practice makes practice*. Forget about perfection. Remember: expecting perfection, even some of the time, guarantees pain. And besides, being perfect would be boring. (I, for one, am proud to say I'm *not* boring.)

Practice expanding your awareness of all the various parts of yourself. Practice disagreeing with the Should Monster. Practice being a Decision Maker. Practice self-forgiveness and accepting personal responsibility. But don't practice to achieve perfection; practice for the sake of practicing. Practice because to do so feels right, makes you feel better about yourself, and maximizes the positive influence you can have on others around you. Practice like a monk practices meditation.

Let go of the illusion of perfection as an attainable goal. Just keep washing the dishes.

> Perfection is not an option today. What a relief!

Practice All Seven Components

Make a list of the seven components of self-forgiveness and put the list where you will see it each morning. (The bathroom mirror usually works.) Review the components each morning for the next couple of weeks. Get accustomed to thinking in terms of the seven components.

Make a conscious decision to apply the seven components to circumstances in your daily life. When you feel stuck or defeated or disappointed or frustrated, think about the seven components and identify which component needs work at that precise moment by asking questions like these:

- Am I allowing the committee to have its say or am I demanding single-mindedness?

- Is the Should Monster at the helm, intimidating me and telling me how to think? Have I slipped back into the habit of believing the gospel according to Should?

- Is my Decision Maker present, and as the Decision Maker am I claiming my rightful authority?

- Am I remembering that perfection is not a choice . . . that practice makes practice?

After a couple of weeks, write a short list of your own reminders to review every morning. Change the list as you grow. Make reviewing your reminder list a daily practice—like brushing your teeth.

Strenuous Rest

One essential aspect of the development of a *daily practice* is learning to relax—letting go of the need to control everything, allowing yourself to go with the flow. If you have a long history of being hard on yourself, relaxing is not such an easy task—even though you *should* be able to relax according to your old friend the Should Monster. In fact, learning to relax is often a more difficult task than identifying the committee and facing your Should Monster combined.

Through the years I have witnessed client after client make excellent progress plowing through the first six components, only to panic when faced with the payoff. When your life is once again—or maybe for the first time—your own, what do you do with it? You may feel like a workaholic suddenly without work. After all, you have spent years heavily involved with your self-criticism. I heard a workshop participant describe it like this:

> I call my Should Monster "the Warden." To cope with his incessant beratement I developed what I think of as "prison mentality." In prison, you adjust your expectations to match the extreme limitations of your environment. Living under the watchful eye of the Warden, I eventually came to accept the nature of my "confinement." I didn't expect much of myself or of the world around me. In prison, a good day is one in which you don't get stabbed.

So like a long-term prisoner recently released, you may not find your newly won freedom all that comforting at first. Just because stressors are relieved, it does not necessarily mean that you will feel less stressed. You may not have spent much time considering what you would do with your life if the Should Monster wasn't in charge. Beginning the important work of discovering who you are as an individual, separate and apart from your Should Monster, can be quite stressful. Give yourself time to adjust to the new organizational structure within you. Your task at this point is to develop some specific ways that you can practice relaxing, giving yourself the necessary time and space to increase your awareness of who you really are and what is really important to you.

Welcoming the Weird

Several years ago, on a late Thursday afternoon, my last client for the day came into the office, sat down, and let out a big sigh. "How are you doing?" I began. Another sigh, and she said, "Weird. This week has been really weird."

I remember this particular session clearly because I was not feeling well myself that day. It was late in the afternoon and late in the work week, and I remember thinking, "this is going to be a tough session and

I'm not sure I have it in me." I was ready to be finished for the day, ready to get out of the world of human conversation and go home to throw a stick for my dog who doesn't even speak English. But Jenny, my last client of the day, had had a weird week, and like it or not, we were going to dive into it now. I shifted in my chair and let out a sigh (hopefully imperceptible to Jenny) of my own.

What followed was, much to my surprise, one of the easiest therapy sessions I have ever experienced—*and* one very important lesson for me . . . and maybe for Jenny.

Jenny had been in therapy in one form or another for about three years. She was a hard-working client, serious about getting better. She had participated in group therapy for the best part of a year in conjunction with her regular individual sessions and occasional relationship therapy. She had even taken a month off from work—no small matter for this highly productive, perfectionistic professional woman—to attend an intensive residential therapy program. You might say that she was more than serious; she was hell-bent on getting better.

"What brand of weird?" I asked her, just after my (hopefully) subtle sigh.

Jenny began to describe her week. Other than the standard therapeutic nods and occasional comments to let her know that I was paying attention, I didn't have much to do for the next hour. She told about two or three interactions at work that left her feeling "weird." She told about an "extremely weird" week with her boyfriend. She even threw in a "strange" telephone conversation with her mother. Most of our sessions had been interactional, but this day Jenny talked almost nonstop. "This is weird," I thought to myself.

But Jenny was a good consumer of my services, and she wasn't going to let me off the hook entirely. She paused when there were about ten minutes left in the session, and asked, "So what do you think?"

I smiled, probably even laughed, because I was happy to tell her what I thought. Tired or not, I had not had the slightest difficulty listening to Jenny that day. What I heard was good news: Every single story she had told, every episode that had contributed to her "weird" week, was a story in which Jenny had taken good care of herself. Jenny had given example after example of positive self-representation. Unlike her past tendency to give her personal power away to others, she was acting from a position of personal strength, and more importantly, from a sense of positive self-esteem. She wasn't second-guessing herself at every turn. Her previously very powerful Should Monster was having little to say about what she did, what she said, and how she said it. The Should Monster was still right there with her—she seemed very clear about that— but it didn't have the credibility or the strength it once had. As I listened to Jenny describe her "weird" week, I realized that she was not only disagreeing with her Should Monster (and even with her mother), she was doing so automatically. She had passed into the land of unconscious competence. And it felt . . . "weird."

Quite simply, Jenny had never had any experience with feeling this good about herself, and especially with maintaining that positive sense of self in the midst of her day-to-day life. And what was brand new to her would of course feel "weird."

We both laughed as I was offering my observations and interpretations of what she had told me. It was a time of relief, and of celebration. I, for one, felt much better; I wasn't tired at all. And that last session of the day that I had dreaded ran over by at least twenty minutes because I'd lost track of the time.

Divine Emptiness

That particular session with Jenny taught me an important lesson. Since then, I have come to recognize the significance of the word "weird," as well as its cousins, "strange" and "foreign." I am still amazed—and entertained—by how often my clients use these specific words when they begin to really apply what they have been learning in therapy. Of course, I still listen for the exceptions, but far more often than not, when I hear one of these words early in a session, I sit back and relax, knowing that this is going to be fun.

I was telling this story to a therapy group once when a young man said, "That's easy for you to say. But good news or not, moving into that new, uncharted 'foreign' territory is scary." And the young man was absolutely right, and his confrontation has become an essential addendum to my Jenny lesson.

When you do the nitty-gritty work of applying the seven components of self-forgiveness to your life, the result will more than likely be admission into a *strange, weird, and foreign* territory in which you will feel at a loss to understand what is happening, not to mention how best to respond. Here is an excellent description a client gave of this experience:

> *I understand that I am experiencing the "payoff" for all of the hard work I have been doing, but I don't know what to do next. I don't know what to do with myself. It's like my old ways of dealing with things—criticizing myself, being instantly angry with myself or someone else—have been cleared out, but I don't have anything to replace them with. The scary part is that feeling of emptiness, like I'm in a state of limbo.*

I was particularly struck by this client's description of this as "emptiness." I liked the idea that so much of what has been toxic has been cleared out. And I have come to think of this experience as *divine emptiness*.

When you get there, it will probably take you a little while to realize exactly where you are (hence, the weirdness), but even when you do, the eerie feeling will not just go away. Give it time. Give yourself time. Don't rush to fill the emptiness. Let yourself become familiar with it, even to celebrate the progress that it represents.

And try not to be too put off by the fear you might experience. I have a friend who says, "You know it's *divine emptiness* if it scares the *hell* out of you."

The Power of Not Knowing

Most of us have come to fear the state of "not knowing." To "not know" is equated with having no control, and it is generally regarded as anything but progress. ("I don't know what's next . . . I don't know what to do now that I am ready to stop beating myself up and holding myself back. I don't know who I will be when I finally do let go of these unforgiving beliefs about myself. I don't know and I am afraid.")

"I don't know" is the state of divine emptiness. The eastern philosophy of Zen teaches us the value of *not knowing*. Zen teaches us to maintain a "beginner's mind," reminding us that the expert has nothing to learn; the beginner has everything to learn.

Adopt the philosophy of *beginner's mind* and the *not knowing* that once frightened you becomes the empty space full of your potential to learn, and to grow.

Knowing what you want is not
a prerequisite for deserving it.

Think of the empty space that you have created by separating your true identity from interpretations, beliefs, and directives that are toxic to you, as a big empty room—*your* big empty room.

You have cleared the space of all its previous furnishings in order to make room for the furnishings (beliefs) of your choice. This is your space and you have worked hard to create this emptiness. Resist the temptation to fill the space immediately, even when the openness, the *not knowing*, scares you.

Try sitting in the very center of your empty room. Sit in each of the corners, or dance, or turn a cartwheel. Most importantly, give yourself credit for your accomplishment. If you have trouble doing that, throw your Should Monster out of *your* room. Sure, it will wait just outside the door, or even peek in the windows, but it cannot come in unless you let it in. Claim your space. Stake your claim, your right to *not know* what comes next.

Journal Exercise

I Don't Know

Without giving it much thought, make a quick list of "I don't knows." Write as quickly as the phrases come to mind: *I don't know why . . . , I don't know what . . . , I don't know how . . . , I don't know if. . . .*

At the end of your list, write the following words in big, bold letters:

AND I DON'T HAVE TO KNOW!

Or shout those same words at the top of your lungs. I DON'T HAVE TO KNOW!

Filling the Space

When I first went into business for myself, I rented a two-room, hole-in-the-wall place on Music Row here in Nashville. Looking back, that little office was very small and quite ugly. It had some kind of imitation wood paneling that was made to look like tree bark. One wall, in the smaller of the two rooms, was covered in red wallpaper with black pinstripes. But that space wasn't ugly to me then—in fact, it was *beautiful*. It was *mine*, and *I loved it*.

Those two little rooms were also completely empty. I had just quit what turned out to be my last "real job" to open my private psychotherapy practice. The last thing I needed to do was spend a lot of money on office furniture. Besides, I didn't have the money (or the credit) to furnish the place even if I had wanted to.

That office represented my potential. It was a scary thing to do, sort of like jumping blindfolded off a cliff, but I had taken the plunge . . . and I had landed in a little two-room office on 16th Avenue South, Nashville, Tennessee. It was my open space, my *divinely empty* space.

I had the telephone installed and hooked up my new answering machine—they both sat on the floor. I counted my money—that didn't take long—and then I thought about furniture. I figured that since I sat and talked with people for a living, the only furniture absolutely necessary was chairs.

I drove over to a nearby antique shop and found three old chairs that I liked. Within a week, I had eight fairly comfortable wooden chairs in a circle in the larger room of my two-room office. A group therapist was born; I had begun to fill my space with items of *my choice*.

Even those first choices turned out to be a bit hasty. Two or three of the chairs were not as sturdy as I had thought, and I spent a few therapy sessions somewhat distracted from what my clients were saying— I was watching the chairs in hopes that the joints I had recently glued would hold.

I rented that first office over a dozen years ago. The office I occupy today is reasonably larger than that first office, and I share an office suite with three other friends and colleagues. But my personal space, *my office*, still consists of two rooms. There is no bark wall paneling and no red wall with black pinstripes. And the place is completely furnished, furnished with items of my choice.

Even when I began to see a financial return from my original investment of eight chairs, I didn't rush out to purchase office furniture. By that time I had developed a habit of perusing the local antique shops, looking for "stuff" that I wanted to put in my space.

Just about anything you could point out in my office today—be it sofa, chair (all very sturdy), end table, lamp, or knickknack—has a story that goes with it. I gathered the items over time and brought them "home" to my space. Doing it that way was the greatest lesson of patience I have ever experienced. And the good feeling I have every time I walk into my office tells me that the result was well worth the wait. My office is a collection of me.

Your Space

The gradual furnishing of my office has become an excellent metaphor that reminds me to slow down and experience the emptiness rather than obeying the reflex to fill it at once. I seem to need that reminder again and again; and there is nothing wrong with needing to be reminded.

Create your own metaphor or image that will remind you to slow down and experience the emptiness. Become willing to not only acknowledge, but to celebrate, your hard work, the clearing out of what has been toxic to you. A friend of mine says that the celebration is every bit as important as the journey. I think she is right, especially for those of us who have been so unforgiving of ourselves. For us, learning to celebrate ourselves becomes the toughest challenge of all.

Remain steadfast. Protect your emptiness from the toxic beliefs that will try to reenter the space. Remain alert and aware. Watch for the beliefs that you want, and invite them into your space. Think your new thoughts. Practice your new beliefs, even before you believe them. Act according to your new thoughts. Behave toward yourself with love and respect— make this your daily practice, your daily commitment. And when you lose your place (as we all will), practice self-forgiveness: get up, brush yourself off, ask for some help, laugh a little, do whatever is called for, and then begin again.

Expect Results

One of the side effects of self-help work and psycho-therapy is that in learning that "life is a journey, not a destination," you can become complacent with *never arriving*. I prefer to think of life as a journey with many destinations. As long as you keep traveling, you have every right to expect to keep arriving.

After all, my kitchen is spotless right now . . . I think.

When you feel the Should Monster pushing in on you, remind your perfectly imperfect self of this essential slogan: Practice makes . . . practice.

Points of Reference

- Each day renew your commitment to being on your own side.

- Knowing when you don't know something is not an admission of weakness or inadequacy; it is a reflection of open-mindedness and humility.

PART III

The Troubleshooters

What we call failure is just a mechanism through which we can learn to do things right.

—Deepak Chopra, M.D.,
Creating Affluence

12

The Power of Persistence

Written in plain old black magic marker, but matted and framed rather nicely, there are four words hanging on the wall behind his desk: *Persistence is what counts.* He is a writer friend of mine, and from where I stand, he is the personification of the magic marker words behind his desk.

I remember the first conversation I ever had with my writer friend, Robert. "Talent's good, and skill, that comes with time. There is only one thing you absolutely have to have if you are serious about being a writer."

"Paper?" An involuntary, smart-alec hiccup from me.

"That too. But I'm talking about persistence. *If you refuse to quit*—no matter what—*you will succeed.* Who knows what that success will look like; every one of us is different. But I will guarantee you: *persistence pays.*"

There's no counting the number of times I have passed Robert's advice on to friends, clients, workshop participants, and fellow writers. I guess you could say that I am very persistent about passing on this powerful pearl of wisdom. (Alliteration not intended.)

Sometimes I worry that I am overemphasizing the importance of Robert's advice, but so far I cannot see that I am. When something doesn't come naturally, when first attempts are frustrated, when second and third attempts are fumbled, there is one more essential ingredient that must be packed for the trip. It is persistence.

Persistence Pays

When you get down to the core of whatever problems introduced you to therapy, support groups, or self-help material, you will be face to face with . . . *yourself*. The part of you that is hurting and wants to change faces the part of you that in many ways has been indiscriminately learning from day one, soaking up life's experiential lessons like a sponge, and now acting as an intricately programmed computer that has developed a will of its own. What was it my father used to say? "Nobody said it was going to be easy."

Hopefully, the previous eleven chapters have given you some practical tools that will help initiate the changes that you want to make. And maybe some of my thoughts have sparked some of your own ideas that will help to lead you out of habitual, ineffective, and often destructive self-criticism and toward that daily practice of self-compassion. And hopefully you have made, or are in the process of making, a solid, life-changing decision to *go for it*—come hell or high water, as they say.

If so, I would like to pass on a bit of wisdom that I heard from a friend several years ago, a bit of wisdom that has been reinforced again and again in my life, a bit of wisdom that I believe tells a great deal about the secret of success. No, I don't expect to surprise you with this, but I do want you to know that I mean every word:

I will guarantee you—persistence pays.

Facing the Threats

To persist you must remain positive, but realistic. You must be able to sincerely expect the best, and be ready to handle the worst. You must be able to look that old Threat Monster in the eye, and say, loud and clear, "I am willing to take the risk," to whatever the latest *If . . . then . . .* threat is. For example, Threat Monster: "If you stand up for yourself in this situation, your family is going to be very angry with you." You: "My intention is not to make anyone angry, but I am willing to take that risk."

This, by the way, is the only way to successfully face the Threat Monster. Beware of the "old program" temptation to seek reassurance by arguing that whatever is threatened is not going to happen. For example, "No, I don't believe you. My family will not be mad at me." Since you really have no way to predict with 100 percent accuracy how others will respond, the reassurance in this response is weakened.

The Snags

The Threat Monster, the Should Monster, the Cynic, the Pouter, the Hopeless One, the Distracter, or whoever else might be currently sitting on your committee, are only a few of the obstacles that you may encounter on

---

Journal Exercise

Facing the Threat Monster

Read *aloud* each of the "You" responses from several times ("I'm willing to take the risk," and "I don't believe that will happen"). Experience what the difference is for you.

Write some of the threats you have encountered, or expect to encounter, from your Threat Monster. Then write two or three responses to each threat; find the ones that feel the most empowering.

Practice, practice, practice.

---

your way to self-forgiveness. As your committee argues, or members take turns being in control (one day you feel strong and ready for anything; the next day—or the next hour—you feel defeated, ready to give up), there may be people around you who think you have gone crazy. They point out your *strange behavior* (a.k.a. self-care) to one another, theorizing that you have been reading too many of "those" books, or maybe that shrink is actually making things worse.

Or maybe as you so-call "improve yourself," you feel alone, isolated from the world you have come from, and yet not able to reach the new world where you want to be—stranded in limbo. You may even begin to question if that new improved you is really a possibility. Maybe you feel stuck in some other way. Maybe you are discouraged, or sidetracked, or just feel lost.

There are any number of snags you may find along the way. Or maybe they find you.

Introducing the Troubleshooters

What follows is a series of chapters to help you better handle common problems along this road less traveled. These chapters contain information, additional exercises, and experiments that I have gathered through the years in the work with my clients, as they have encountered their snags. As with the material presented in parts I and II, I encourage you to utilize this information as it best suits you. Don't settle for something right off the rack if you can do better with your own creative tailoring.

Each chapter begins with a brief statement of *the problem* you may be encountering, *the need* that arises from that problem, and *the help* that is necessary. You may choose to read straight through these chapters, or you can refer to them as you encounter your snags—like how you use the manual for your VCR.

Journal Exercise

Maintaining Control

Make a list of the committee members that you expect will offer the most resistance to your change. Try having an open committee meeting sometime, with you as the Decision Maker making notes about what everyone has to say. Practice listening to them all, while you maintain the control of the discussion.

What are some of the additional *snags* you expect to encounter along your path to self-forgiveness? Include *feelings* you think may be difficult for you, as well as *people and circumstances* that may (intentionally or not) offer resistance when it becomes apparent that you are thinking and behaving differently. For example: "fear of my own anger," "my husband's need to be in control," "my tendency to back off after I have asserted myself," "the family reunion this Thanksgiving."

Since there is no way to anticipate every problem that every reader will encounter, read for what applies to you and your circumstance, and don't worry if some part just doesn't fit. (Those VCR manuals always include some instructions for a model that you don't own.) You may discover that a particular troubleshooting chapter is overstated for your purposes. Or it may seem understated. In these cases, use your journal writing to create an appropriately adjusted version of the relevant information. Always remember that the words you write in your journal are far more important than the words in this book.

Now, it's time to do some troubleshooting . . .

All things are possible—meaning *all things*. The potential exists for devastating outcomes. The potential exists for extremely positive outcomes. Infinite potentialities wait between the two. In becoming fully responsible for ourselves, we must accept the full range of possibilities. To do otherwise would be settling for something less than whole.

Hide from nothing, and let nothing hide from you.

13

Finding Your Inner Parent

The Problem: "I feel ready, willing, and able to become the Decision Maker in my own life—in theory. But when I attempt to put it into practice, I feel overwhelmed with feelings of shame, guilt, and fear. I understand that these are leftover feelings from my 'old programming,' but knowing that doesn't seem to help much. I'm stopped in my tracks; I feel like a helpless child."

The Need: The Decision Maker needs a major assist in order to do its job, and that helpless child must not be ignored, pushed aside, or relegated to the back of the line.

The Help: It's time to discover the Parent Within.

Your Inner Child

As the Decision Maker, your job can be pretty difficult if you are flooded with emotional pain, and/or a frightening sense of vulnerability that frequently results when defenses are dropped, and you are taking a good, long look inside. It may feel like you are trying to renovate your home while it's on fire.

Those vulnerable, painful, and sometimes confusing feelings tend to show up just when you think you are starting to feel better. And in fact, that is exactly what is happening. The long-buried emotions will emerge when you have done enough work to make your world a safer place. Picture a child peaking around the door to the basement, where the child has been hiding for the past how-ever-many years.

The Decision Maker needs some help, and the child emerging from the basement needs a parent.

The Child in Disguise

For many years now we have been hearing about the importance of discovering the child within us. For thousands and thousands of people this simple metaphor has been the key that has opened the door to emotional, spiritual, and even physical healing. But, discovering the child part is not all that difficult. Most of us have spent the majority of our adult lives feeling like twelve-year olds (or eight-year-olds, or four-year-olds) walking around in disguise, ever fearful of the dreaded day when someone would recognize that we are not adults at all—but children masquerading as adults.

We tend to view ourselves through our twelve-year-old eyes, seeing everyone else as having it all together and being the "real adults," while we, on the other hand, are mere impostors.

Journal Exercise

Being an Adult

Write your definition for "being an adult."

In what ways do you—or have you—felt like an impostor in your personal or professional life? In what ways do you have difficulty (no matter how old you are) perceiving yourself as an adult?

"And so," I tell my clients who have experienced the miracle of recovering their lost inner child, "the more difficult task is yet to come: Discovering the Parent Within."

The Child in the Basement

While the "impostor" child has been masquerading through your day-to-day life, keeping everything afloat, the emotionally loaded basement kid has remained out of sight and (as much as possible) out of mind. The "impostor" child needs a parent, but can take pretty good care of him- or herself. After all, the "impostor" is a survivor, a tough kid. The child in the basement brings an urgency to it all; this child needs attention . . . NOW.

The basement-child within represents something more than the stereotypical playful, carefree elements of our personalities. This child holds pain and cries out with needs—legitimate needs that were not met during chronological childhood. This type of inner child is an emotionally wounded, vulnerable part of each of us, a part that we all at one time or another attempt to hold at arm's length, afraid of the repercussions of accepting the needs and pain as our own.

In a nutshell, we find this child crying on the doorstep of our psyche and haven't the faintest idea what to do.

Rejecting the Child Within

A normal and common response to the child-within metaphor is not wanting to have anything to do with the child, or better yet, to reject the metaphor as silly, refusing to acknowledge the vulnerable and frightening feelings associated with it.

I remember a client in group therapy who was introduced to the child metaphor through a guided visualization. She described her feelings for the child like this: "It's hard to tell if I fear her or hate her more. She disgusts me. I don't even want to look at her. And I sure don't want to go anywhere near her."

The same client also described how she felt about herself during and after the guided visualization: "I feel completely ashamed of myself. I know that I am supposed to love the child in me, but I don't. I am as disgusted with myself as I am with her."

This seemed like a no-win situation to my client: She was very much in touch with genuine feelings, but she believed the feelings she was having were wrong. In essence, it was difficult to define this client's emotional experience in adult terms at all. In the visualization she had seen a child so full of pain and unmet needs that she had instinctively rejected her, and then she (the adult client) felt like a scolded and shamed child herself. She was rejecting herself for rejecting the child. This is an excellent example of how quickly and effectively the Should Monster can go to work. Once she had stepped into the quicksand of shame, there were no positive, reassuring thoughts to be found in her consciousness. Her Should Monster had pounced on the opportunity to remind her of what a "bad person she really is."

Her Decision Maker, not having previously known about the child in the basement, was completely unable to function.

Having said that, believe it or not, some of us go looking for the child within. We expend great amounts of energy, time, and money to return to the child and to the child's buried feelings. Of course, we do so with high hopes of healing our psychic pain.

Others I have known—like my client—do not have to go looking for their child. The child finds them, sometimes bursting through the basement door, screaming, "Help! I can't stay down there anymore!" These people will at first hope to expend their energy getting that child back down into the basement. However, it is unlikely the child will co-operate, and even if the child does, it is probably too late. The secret is out; the hidden picture has been spotted. There is *something* in the basement, and now there is no denying it.

Your Inner Parents

The Should Parent

A child within calls for a parent within. The problem that most of us face is that the nearest thing to an inner parent that we have experienced is tyrannical and full of *shoulds, oughts,* and *shame on yous.* In other words: The Should Monster.

Since most of us have been under the care and supervision of these dominating, impossible-to-please, compulsive tyrants since childhood, we again have our work cut out for us. With the discovery of the child within, we are once more challenged to recognize the old messages of the Should Monster for what they are—in this case, outdated and ineffective self-parenting.

The Positive Parent Within

Remember from the earlier chapters: we don't need to be rid of what is negative as much as we need to face it, recognize it for what it is, even accept it (not the same as agreeing with it). Then, we can turn our attention to more important matters. We don't need to *exorcise* the negative. We need to *exercise* the positive. In this case I'm referring to the Positive Parent Within.

Journal Exercise

The Should-Monster Parent

Describe your Should Monster as a parent. What kinds of things does it do and say (as a parent) that are hurtful to the child within you? What are some of the needs of your inner child that are ignored and neglected by the Should-Monster Parent?

As children we needed more than anything for our parents to be benevolent powers greater than us. We needed to experience our own power, our own magnificent child energy within the safety of parental containment—safe containment; a place for us to explore, experiment, and expand. We needed parents who would neither overpower us nor be overpowered by us. The parents' mission was to create and maintain physical and emotional safety in which a child could grow successfully. Power struggles to demonstrate "who is boss" or an inability to stand firm when a child was doing the important work of testing limits, would ultimately be counterproductive.

The preceding paragraph is a description of healthy parents who can let a child's life be about the child; who can take their responsibilities completely seriously and give the child plenty of room to grow. To the degree that we received positive parenting like this in childhood, we are self-caring adults. To the degree that positive parenting that was needed was not available—for whatever reasons—or negative, critical, or abusive parenting was provided, we will have established similar negative, critical, abusive, or absent habits of self-care.

No two people, even from the same family, will have the same history in this regard. We are all unique. And each of us has the responsibility to face whatever we must face in order to become the self-caring adults we are capable of being.

This is done by pulling what has too long been hidden—even from ourselves—out of the dark corners of our consciousness (the basement), by exploring and ultimately accepting what is true, and by making conscious choices to practice, one day at a time, being the loving and powerful parent our inner child needs.

A Brand New You

After doing the Child-Sitting Experiment and spending two weeks being with, and speaking with, your child-self, you will probably move through a considerable amount of the awkward, embarrassed feelings. If your child is in need of a new parent, your relationship with the child will initially feel strange and unfamiliar. By the end of the two-week period, your new role as Inner Parent may begin to feel more comfortable. And your Decision Maker will have a new, much needed ally.

When you are using this experiment, you are building up the strength of a brand new part of you. This is not your mother, or your father, or your Should Monster. You have planted a magical seed. To water and nurture this seed, all you need is to practice. This is a daily practice of being a quality parent to a wonderful, deserving child.

This can be the beginning of a beautiful relationship.

Experiment
Child-Sitting

Week 1: Find a photograph of yourself as a child. You may want to look through many old photographs to help you reconnect to feelings from your early life, but eventually decide on one photo of your child-self to use in this exercise. (If you do not have access to photographs of your childhood—or if none exist—draw a simple picture to represent your child-self.)

Put your photograph or drawing in a special and safe place in your home. You may even choose to put a nice frame on your picture. Treat it well.

For the next week, once a day, go to your special, safe place and sit with your photograph. Sit silently with your child for about five minutes. Practice seeing the child in the picture as separate from you (the adult). Breathe deeply and gently, practicing simple awareness of this "relationship within."

Week 2: Continue the exercise as above with one addition: After sitting silently with your picture for a minute or two, speak to your child. Each day for the next week, speak aloud to the child represented by your photograph or drawing. This may seem awkward or silly, but try it anyway. (I'll never tell.) Speak directly to the child in the present tense, and speak as an adult to a child. Say whatever is in your heart.

Journal Writing: This is an excellent exercise to incorporate into your writing. If you do so, I suggest that you not write during the meditation (the time with your child), but immediately following. You could write about what you said to your inner child, how you felt about the experience, or even what you think your child would say back. Simply write about whatever comes to mind.

14

Returning the Emotional Flow

The Problem: "I've been holding back and swallowing feelings for so long that I'm not sure I know how to express my feelings. Sometimes I'm not sure that I even know how I feel. I do know how it feels to be emotionally shut down; I think I know how it feels to feel nothing."

The Need: The natural flow of emotional experience and expression needs restoring. It's very important that both of these aspects (experience and expression) be addressed.

The Help: It's time to place an emphasis on learning to identify, respect, and express emotions.

The Emotional Flow

We seem to trust our physical bodies, at least to some extent. For instance, we seldom (if ever) question the natural flow of our digestive system. We eat. We drink. We digest. We expel the waste after absorbing the fuel.

We repeat this vital, natural cycle for entire lifetimes without much conscious thought, and without critical interference from our own minds.

(As you read this, if you have an eating disorder, you may notice that this is not true for you; that you do experience critical interference in regard to your digestive system. I invite you to proceed with this analogy anyway and apply what follows to your physical digestive system as well as your system of emotional flow.)

We share the common understanding that our digestive system is designed as a *one-way track*. To reverse the direction of this system, to block the flow, even to hurry the system (unnecessary use of laxatives) goes against this design. For the sake of this discussion, let's agree that we share this healthy respect for our physical digestive process.

Respect for our physicalness is essential to our health. We are also emotional, mental, and some would say, spiritual beings. We tend to have respect for our mental functioning above all else. We tend to compartmentalize our spiritual nature when we even acknowledge it; and we tend to *abuse ourselves emotionally*. This abuse, based on erroneous beliefs, most often takes the form of attempts to block and/or reverse the flow of our natural *emotional digestive system*.

Emotional Constipation

Here is a highly simplified, yet pertinent psychology lesson:

Just as we ingest food physically, we live in a world of external experience, constantly taking in (ingesting) that experience. Though we do not question our right (and the necessity) of relieving ourselves by regularly using the rest room, we are constantly questioning our right to allow ourselves natural expression of our emotional responses to "ingesting" experience. If I feel the need to urinate, I don't find myself lost in inner dialogue asking, "Have I really taken in enough fluid to justify this need? Do I really deserve to use the rest room?" Such inner dialogue, of course, sounds ridiculous, and would be a needless use of my valuable mental energy. We do, however, seem to waste plenty of that valuable mental energy questioning our right to express feelings, and even our right to have the feelings in the first place. The result, quite simply, is *emotional constipation*—a build-up of years and years of unexpressed emotional responses to living in a world of external experience.

The problem of this emotional constipation is compounded by two facts. First, unexpressed, stored emotions are no longer easily associated with specific events from our past. We lose the ability to connect *one feeling* with *one experience*, and with that, we all too often tell ourselves that unless we can mentally make that precious connection, we had better not express ourselves. Second, we live in a society that attaches emotional expression to blame, we helplessly abide by an erroneous law of life that dictates: "If I do not have a justifiable target for my emotional release, I had better keep my feelings to myself."

We find ourselves lost to the legalistic thinking that in order to have, admit to, and express a feeling (especially the feeling we call anger) we must prove beyond all reasonable doubt that we have been unfairly victimized. In our efforts to be responsible, we wisely want to avoid the mind-set of victimization, and so we are left holding the emotional bag. Unfortunately, we hold this "emotional bag" inside our minds and bodies where it can do the most damage.

In brief, we find ourselves helplessly constipated, living in a world of experience that we cannot help but "ingest." And yet, our options for release of and relief from this natural energy called emotion are dramatically limited by our own ineffective belief systems.

Let It Flow

"No, no, no . . . you don't want me to uncork this constipated reservoir of emotion. Once I started, there would be no stopping me. And besides, people could get hurt."

If you are emotionally constipated, you can safely bet that at one time in your life, blocking, swallowing, minimizing, and blatantly denying feelings was the wisest choice you could make. Give yourself some credit. And it seems reasonable that now, if you are considering letting go of the need to control the flow of natural emotion, you will be wary of attempting such a drastic change. After all, if you are experiencing emotional constipation, it is highly unlikely that you had teachers in your past who modeled healthy, appropriate expression of feelings. You will be lacking lots of "how-tos." When this is the case, it is important to simply acknowledge that *you don't know how.*

Human Emotion 101

Where there is emotional constipation, there will be a deficit of self-acceptance. In fact, there is no more powerful way to stop the natural flow of emotion than to stand in judgment of our feelings.

Think back to the exercises in chapter 8, where you explored the lessons learned in your alma mater family. What were the family policies (spoken or unspoken) regarding feelings? Were emotions globally considered either good or bad? Were some feelings more acceptable than others? Were some feelings definite no-nos? Were there double standards as in, "It's okay for me, but not for you, to be angry"?

The implication of so many rules and regulations about emotions is that you are—or you *should* be—in control of what you feel at all times. This completely unrealistic expectation is one of the primary set-ups for a lifetime of self-condemnation. Lessons learned about the acceptability and unacceptability of certain emotions become fertile ground for Should Monsters to grow.

Journal Exercise

The Committee's Policies on Emotion

Write your Should Monster's policy regarding emotions. Write in the second person for this (that is, He believes . . . , She insists . . .) to help *reduce your identification* with your Should Monster.

Write your Decision Maker's policy regarding emotions. Write this in the first person (I believe . . .) in order to *increase your identification* with the Decision Maker.

The truth that we need to know—and are not often taught—is that everyone has the capacity for *all* human emotions, and those emotions are neither good nor bad in and of themselves. Ethical and moral opinions apply to how we choose to express our feelings, not to the feelings themselves. If a child's only experience with a certain feeling is negative (either from witnessing unhealthy or destructive expression, or from being told that he or she is wrong or bad when expressing particular feelings), the result will be an unforgiving attitude toward having that feeling, and ultimately toward him- or herself.

Lesson #1 of Human Emotion 101 is that *all feelings are acceptable.* We have the ability to greatly influence how we feel by changing the ways we interpret the world we live in, but no one is, or needs to be, totally in control of their feelings. Feelings just are. They exist neither in the past nor the future, only in the present. What we call "old" feelings are feelings born out of past events that have not found adequate expression. At any given time, feelings either have or have not been expressed. They exist only in the present tense.

Lesson #2 is that *each of us is responsible for effectively identifying our feelings, and making healthy choices about how to express them satisfactorily.* When we have not previously learned how to do so, it is our responsibility to find a way to learn.

By accepting the full range of feelings within ourselves, and by acting responsibly in our choices of expression, we will begin to build a new relationship with our natural, human emotions. We can forgive ourselves for having the so-called negative feelings in the first place; we do this by recognizing that in this regard, there is literally nothing to forgive. And we can become students of emotional expression, learning satisfying and ethical ways to communicate at an emotional level with others.

By learning better ways to express feelings, we increase our options—and our abilities—for addressing emotionally charged miscommunication. In other words, we become more capable and proficient at responding to the natural guilt that tell us when apology and correction are called for. Being fully responsible for ourselves, remember, is an absolute necessity if we intend to forgive ourselves all along the way.

From Existence to Expression

Emotions will pose a threat to us for as long as we avoid facing them, and for as long as we side step the responsibility of learning how to effectively express them. Unresolved emotions are the accumulated "stuff" in the garage (or attic)—you know, the stuff that we have always intended to do something with, but just never got around to it.

For a while—sometimes a very long while—we can just look the other way when we have to walk through the garage. Later, we can avoid going into the garage altogether if that's what it takes. But sooner or later we must face the task, usually when we have decided to move out of one place and into another. (I love it when a metaphor comes together.)

Experiment

Emotional X Ray

Find a quiet place to sit, breathing deeply and gently, tuning in to your emotional stuckness or constipation. You may have a particular emotion in mind, or you may just follow your intuition to lead you to a constipated spot. Remain particularly aware of your physical body—you will most likely feel the blocked emotion there first. (For example, a knot in the stomach, a constriction at the throat, tightness in the center of the chest, sensation in the arms or legs, a headache, and so on.)

Once you locate the constipation, remain in quiet meditation with it for a minute or two more. Do not attempt to alter the stuckness; simply experience it. Imagine that you can see it in your body. See it, feel it, even hear it if it speaks or makes sounds. Trust your imagination and intuition. You cannot do this exercise wrong.

Now use a sheet of paper and some markers or crayons to draw a picture of your experience of the constipated emotion. Draw whatever comes to mind. If you are unsure how to start, simply draw a picture of your body with the stuck emotion(s) in it. Use your nondominant hand to draw the picture. That is, if you are right-handed, use your left hand and vice versa. This will allow you to let go of any artistic perfectionism that you have and it will actually help access a closer connection to the feeling part or yourself.

When we can get beyond the attempts to ignore, deny, or distract from our feelings, we can roll up our sleeves and focus on the task at hand: reinstating the emotional flow. This will be accomplished by identifying and accepting the truth about the neglected garage, and learning new and better ways of expressing (releasing) both the stored emotions associated with events of the past, and the emotions associated with our here-and-now, daily lives.

Emotional Expression 101

In the realm of emotional *experience*, self-forgiveness makes sense only in terms of self-acceptance. Faced with the existence of the feelings themselves, there is simply nothing to forgive. We all possess the capacity to experience a full range of feelings. It's a fact, like breathing air.

Certainly with honest introspection and a willingness to change, we can greatly influence *how* and *what* we feel by learning healthier, more realistic ways to interpret our experiences. In this, we do the best we can do, keeping in mind that to stand in judgment of an emotion as either good or bad is about as helpful as deciding that the waste that will result from the digestion of an unhealthy meal should not be allowed to leave the body because it is somehow wrong.

Emotional *expression* is another matter. Here, the rules do apply. It is the responsibility of each of us to identify emotional experience and make decisions about how we'll express those emotions. These decisions do need to be judged by some ethical standard—the standard known as our own *personal value system*. When we fail to make good decisions in this regard, and emotional expression falls outside the bounds of our personal value system, we will experience *natural guilt*. Remember, this is the helpful guilt (a.k.a. conscience) that will appropriately police our behavioral choices, pointing us back in the right direction when we veer off course. This natural guilt operates within us all (at least anyone who would be inclined to read this book), and will increase in effectiveness as we separate from the neurotic guilt inspired by the Should Monster.

Remember the discussion about the two guilts in Chapter 3? *Natural guilt* says, "I act in a way that is in violation of my personal value system. Consequently, I feel the discomfort that sooner or later I recognize as guilt. I make amends and corrections in whatever ways are possible; these actions are fueled by the guilt. Within a short amount of time, I experience relief; the guilt has passed." *Neurotic guilt* says, "I may or may not act in a way that is in violation of my personal value system, but somehow I sense that I have done something wrong. I feel the discomfort that I recognize as guilt, a feeling that I consider to be a consistent part of my emotional makeup. I ruminate about the feelings and any circumstances that lead to my feelings, or I attempt to avoid the feelings. Sooner or later I may or may not make amends and corrections in the ways that are available to me; these actions, when I choose to act, are fueled by

---

Journal Exercise

The Two Guilts

Which description of guilt do you identify with most? From the general descriptions above, write about how *you* specifically experience natural and neurotic guilt. Beware of the either/or trap. Rather than asking yourself, "Do I have natural or neurotic guilt?" ask the more productive question of "How do I experience each kind of guilt?"

---

shame. Afterward, I may feel some relief, but very soon I will be haunted by the discomfort of residual guilt."

Since rules do apply, here are a few fundamental guidelines that can be helpful as you practice the strange, new custom of honest emotional expression:

It Shows, So Tell

There are countless ways to avoid expressing emotions directly, and just as many reasons to rationalize why it is better to take that long way around. We could hurt someone's feelings or make someone mad at us for instance. Or our perceptions of what happened could be mistaken. (For example, you might tell yourself, "Maybe it was an oversight and not an intentional act on the part of my colleague. Given the possibility that I could be wrong, it seems a much more prudent decision to keep my feelings to myself. I'll just toss them in the garage with the others ... I really must get around to cleaning out that garage some day. Maybe next weekend.")

The feelings we are not speaking are probably attempting some way to express themselves—plotting an escape—on their own. It's as if the feelings themselves have a desire to move on through. And so we find ourselves involved in some kind of a tug-a-war with our own feelings. Some of them just won't go peacefully to the garage.

Consider the amount of energy that you might expend, during the course of one year, playing tug-a-war with your feelings. For most of us, we are talking about a funding policy that could make the federal government's seem efficient. And not only are we wasting good energy to protect ourselves and others from our "dangerous" emotions, but our efforts are at least pointless, and probably detrimental. We are left with more unexpressed, unresolved emotional "stuff," and most people around us probably know how we are feeling anyway.

It's not the fact that we have a full range of feelings in our relationships that throws us off, as much as it is our inexperience with direct communication. The more efficient and effective approach is learning to say what we think and feel. And to do so, we'll need a few more guidelines. . . .

Clarify Your Intention/Check Your Aim

Sarah had been coming to individual therapy sessions for about six months when she joined a weekly group that I co-facilitated. I had enjoyed working with Sarah in her individual sessions, and she had made excellent progress, especially in learning to step forward and say what she was feeling. She demonstrated this progress when she expressed her anger with me because I had been slow in getting some material to her that I had promised. I had dropped the ball a couple of times in fulfilling my commitment, and her anger was completely understandable. Best of all, she was expressing it directly to me in a way that not only established her position as legitimate, but also resulted in her anger being heard. I responded with a sincere apology, along with a congratulations for the excellent communication, and we continued from there. Two weeks later, Sarah joined the group.

As a member of the therapy group, Sarah became outspoken, especially in the confrontation of other group members. Her comments were insightful, but her timing and her tact left much to be desired. Increasingly, Sarah told stories about her new abilities to express her feelings to the people in her life—her husband, her sister, her teenage children, even her boss. During this time in group, however, Sarah did not mention any conversations with her highly critical, "impossible-to-please" (Sarah's phrase) mother.

During one group session, someone made an observation, and another posed a question to Sarah. "It seems like you are telling everyone *how you feel* an awful lot lately. And most of the time *how you feel* is angry," one group member said. Another added, "I don't want to play junior psychologist here, but have you considered the possibility that your anger is coming from some place other than the frustrations of your daily life?" Once the ice was broken, the entire group became involved in the discussion, and at least two group members expressed the anger they felt toward Sarah for her frequent confrontations in past sessions.

That was understandably a difficult session for Sarah, but her genuine desire to make good use of her therapy saw her through. Within two more sessions, Sarah was able, with the help of the group, to make some more progress in insight and practice. A productive side effect of the group's work with Sarah was the beginning of an ongoing discussion about the importance of clarifying what intention is behind emotional expression.

What Sarah came to understand was this: The abilities to clearly identify her feelings and to express them directly presented a turning point for her. After she had expressed her anger with me in the individual session, and "the world didn't end," Sarah's confidence began a steady climb. She was like a kid with a new toy at first, as she practiced the model we had developed in one of her sessions:

> **Focus** inward —> **Identify** the feeling —> **Become aware** of the old way of handling (or avoiding the feeling —> **Choose** (and use) a new way to express the feeling —> **Check** the results.

Essentially, she was practicing a set of new behaviors, which is generally a positive intention. But what happened next had happened outside of Sarah's conscious awareness. When she gave herself permission to express feelings directly, she tapped into a store of anger that had gone unexpressed through most of her life. The constipated anger was mostly associated with her "impossible-to-please" mother. Sarah discovered a short time later that her mother had been the catalyst for a major childhood decision to stop expressing herself in the face of any potential conflict because there was no way she could do it "right" in her mother's eyes, no way that she could "win."

So, as an adult, the more Sarah expressed herself—with family and friends and in the group—the more agitated she became. Expression begot expression. The stored anger had found a way to tunnel out. Rather than feeling better, she was feeling worse, for a couple of good reasons: First, she was increasingly feeling angry to the point of fearing that she was losing control, and second, her excessive and fairly clumsy expressions and confrontations had begun to yield critical responses from others that mimicked her mother's criticisms.

Sarah's intention had shifted (unknown to her) from practicing a new set of behaviors that would help her to feel much better about herself to attempting to find targets for her stored anger. There was no malice involved; she was simply seeking the release and relief that she deserved. It was a little tricky helping Sarah to not slip back into self-condemnation when she recognized the shift of intention. I wrote the following on a three-by-five-inch index card for Sarah to carry as a reminder:

> *The feeling is anger. For that, there is nothing to forgive. Where you have erred in your expressions to family and friends, acknowledge your mistakes to them and apologize.*
>
> *Then, forgive yourself the mistakes, remembering that to the aware mind, mistakes are how we learn.*

Sarah, and several other members of the group, then returned to using the model that she and I had developed—with the following improvement: Be sure to check the intention behind the expression. When in doubt, take the time to run it past a trusted friend. The improved model looks like this:

> **Focus** inward —> **Identify** the feeling —> **Become aware** of the old way(s) of handling (or avoiding) the feeling —> **Choose** a new way to express the feeling —> **Check** the intention

behind the chosen expression —→ **Express** the feeling directly —→ **Check** the results

Expression Is a Two-Way Street

One very important guideline to etch into the back of your mind is that if you want to develop communication skills that will serve you well, it is imperative that you listen as well as speak. Listening to others does not require you to agree with them, or to like what they have to say. And listening to others does not insure that they will reciprocate by listening to you.

To effectively practice this guideline, we must let go of the schoolyard mentality of "Teacher, he started it!" Treat all expression as a two-way process regardless of whether or not the other person or persons are playing by the same rules. Learn to resist the temptation to operate at the lowest personal value system. Operate according to your own.

Patience All Around

Don't ever forget—or more realistically, *be consistently reminded*—that you are in *the process* of learning. No one learns without taking risks. No one learns without making mistakes. And no one learns without having to begin from wherever they are. Of course, expect great things of yourself; commit yourself to returning to your natural emotional flow. Be willing to do what it takes to accomplish your goals. But here is a word of warning: *Don't think for a minute that you are in charge of the timing.*

Have patience. Patience is a quiet and powerful expression of compassion.

Journal Exercise

My Value System

Write about your personal value system in regard to interpersonal communication.

Make a list of ways you tend to lose touch with the value system you just described. Do this in a way that is not about putting yourself down, but is about using your past mistakes to plan for the future.

Don't waste your mistakes. Learn!

15

Clarifying the Confusion

The Problem: "I feel like there's too much information. Too many different ways to look at things. Too many exceptions to every rule. Too many unruly characters on my committee. Too many opinions and suggestions from my friends and family. Too many ways to blow it."

The Need: The Decision Maker has slipped a little—or a lot. There is a need to reinforce your identity as separate from your multiple thoughts and feelings (the committee), clarifying the nature of process (as opposed to outcome).

The Help: It's time to get clear about confusion.

This Is Confusing

Confusion is generally thought of as a *feeling*, along with other notable human emotions such as anger, joy, shame, fear, serenity, guilt. On closer examination, however, the experience of confusion appears to be less an emotion, and more an effective means for *avoiding* emotion. As long as I remain *confused*, I will not have to commit to and/or take responsibility for a plan of action, and I can ask other more distressing feelings—like fear, hurt, and sadness—to take their place in line *behind* the more pressing experience of confusion. In other words, confusion is a defense mechanism.

When we feel confused, we feel stuck, and we complain (at least to ourselves) about the frustration of being stuck. Stuck is not fun, but it may well be perceived by certain members of the committee as preferable to taking a risk by making a decision that could be wrong, and/or may result in feelings more painful than confusion.

A friend of mine says that with hindsight, he can see that he remained in a state of confusion for at least two solid years so that he would not have to face the pain of deciding to end his marriage. A client I worked with several years ago would become "overwhelmed" and confused every time we talked in detail about her family life as a child. For quite a while, she and I both were successfully distracted by the confusion, a confusion that was no doubt perceived as preferable to facing the parental abuse that we eventually discovered on the other side of confusion.

Journal Exercise

Confusion

Describe how you generally experience confusion. What is it like mentally? Emotionally? Physically?

List some feelings (and associated circumstances) that you consider *more painful than confusion.*

Are there examples of when you might have unconsciously chosen confusion as a way to avoid or postpone something more frightening or painful? Are you avoiding anything in your life right now by being confused?

A Committee Ruckus

"Being confused" is a direct result of believing the *myth of singularity* discussed in chapter 5. Falling back into that belief is not hard to do, considering how deeply ingrained the belief is in our culture. We are supposed to be so singularly minded that we have only *one opinion* and *one feeling* at a time, and there is only *one "right"* answer to each dilemma we face.

Of course, we have already seen how our minds are multiple in nature. When we attempt to deny that multiplicity, we block the healthy and natural flow of our ever changing identity and remain stranded on the outskirts of self-awareness, in a land known to us all as Confusion.

Imagine it this way: A loud ruckus ensues inside the conference room; the big conference room door is closed, with you standing outside in the hallway. You hear the arguments; you can even feel the thuds and thumps as furniture goes flying across the room; but for some strange reason, you are unable to perceive the conference room door or the room behind it. Instead, you assume that the loud and muffled voices, and the thuds and thumps are coming from within the singular you. "What's going on," a friend asks. "I'm confused," you reply.

Confusion and Feelings

Confusion may not *be* a feeling, but it is certainly *associated* with a number of different feeling experiences. Fear is probably the most common emotion to be linked with confusion. Fear, in its various forms of nervousness, anxiety, panic, or just plain old agitation, escalates around confusion as the Should Monster enters the picture, demanding clarity, insulting you for being so stupid or weak or whatever. Of course, this only serves to intensify the confusion. Imagine that you are doing the Journal Exercise about how you experience confusion. When your pen touches the paper, I lean in, close to your face, and start insulting you, criticizing you efforts, all the while demanding that you hurry to complete the assigned paragraph. Remember, that is the kind of help the Should Monster has to offer when we are confused.

Shame and frustration are a couple more feelings that are frequently associated with confusion. Again, the Should Monster takes advantage of the vulnerability of confusion to shove the shame down our throats. We may be frustrated at our circumstances, but more often than not, when there is a problem with confusion, we are experiencing the great majority of the frustration, and even anger, as directed toward ourselves, for being confused in the first place.

Redefining Confusion

We need a new definition for confusion. We need to pan back and take in the broader view. We need to see our internal circumstances from high up in the press box, as opposed to right in the middle of the playing field. Instead of settling for the idea that confusion is an uncomfortable feeling, let's try describing the experience in a way that makes sense, in a way that is not so ... well, that is not so confusing.

To do so we will use a multilayered view of self: Physical, Emotional, Mental, and Spiritual. I sometimes ask clients to specifically describe their experience with confusion from each of these perspectives. Following is a description of confusion that is a composite of several of my clients' answers.

Confusion is . . .

- **Mentally**—More than one opinion experienced simultaneously that we think of as contradictory. (We tell ourselves that these so-called contradictory opinions cannot or are not supposed to coexist.)

- **Emotionally**—More than one emotion experienced simultaneously that our "mind" tells us are contradictory (for example, anger and guilt), or an emotion that we judge as unacceptable, illogical, or in some way wrong or bad.

- **Physically**—Specific physical sensations such as tension in a particular part of the body, "butterflies" in the stomach, low or high energy, and so on. (It is very useful to learn to identify your own "physical signals" that tell you when you are confused.)

- **Spiritually**—A sense of interference with or disconnection from a sense of purpose or direction. And/or a feeling many describe as being cut off from God or from Intuition.

Utilizing these descriptions, the confusion seems to originate at the mental level. No surprise there. The real problem, however, is not multiple opinions coexisting, but a belief system that dictates that the multiplicity is unacceptable. This belief system shuts down essential "brainstorming" sessions at the mental level that helps us become more fully aware of *all* of our thoughts about any particular subject or dilemma.

Next, the same stifling belief system (valuing thought over emotion) then slows down (or shuts down) emotional experience with "should" and "should not" messages about the feeling responses. Energy is diverted from *experiencing* the feelings to *critiquing* the feelings.

The physical experience of confusion described above (tension, jitters, whatever) is a direct result of emotions being blocked, and the mind being engaged in some kind of no-win isometric exercise. Essentially, the body's symptoms are an attempt to draw attention to the problem. It is functioning exactly the same way it does when there is a physical ailment or injury that needs attention.

The sense of spiritual disconnection from purpose, intuition, or God is again the direct result of the seemingly endless store of "should" messages. Here, the Should Monster tells us not to trust our own instincts, thoughts, or feelings. The reason this experience is so often depicted at the spiritual level is that the result is a severing of the connection between self and self. Have you ever felt cut off from yourself?

And finally, when we are experiencing all of this, the natural consequence is to become self-absorbed to the point of isolation from the support system around us. The confusion can more easily maintain its hold when we are not talking to others about our experience. (Helpful Hint: This is the perfect time to pick up the phone.)

Experiment

From Confusion to Expanded Awareness

Do you ever find yourself approaching a problem in your life as if there is going to be an answer in the back of the book to prove you right or wrong at grading time? What if there isn't an answer in the back of the book? What if there is no grading time? What if there is no book!?!

This experiment is intended to help bypass fear and shame-based beliefs that tell us we are not thinking "right" or feeling "right." Practice any part or all of it to learn to step around that confusion-inducing belief system described above. Practice this experiment, and you will *step out of the land of confusion into the much more roomy expanse of self-awareness.*

Before beginning this experiment, wait for confusion to set in. If you are like me, you won't have to wait long. In a quiet place take some time to tune in to yourself at each of the four levels described previously: Physical, Emotional, Mental, and Spiritual. Take your time; become an observer of yourself at each of these levels. Consider any judgments or critiques of your performance during this exercise as just a part of the constant flow of thoughts at your mental level. Notice them and let them pass.

Having meditated in this way, take four separate sheets of paper (one for each level), and characterize your experience of confusion at each level of self-awareness (Mental, Emotional, and so on). Don't worry about being particularly articulate or creative. Allow your intuition to lead the way as you describe your confusion at each of the four levels. Trust your initial responses.

Describe physical sensations. Draw pictures if you like. List all emotions that you feel. Describe emotional sensations. When you get to your mental level page, as quickly as you can write, list all of the thoughts you observe. You might need extra paper for this one. And finally, draw and/or write a description of your confusion at the level of spirit or intuition.

Now, on a fifth sheet of paper write the following statement:

All that is described and listed here exists within me. . . . THERE IS ROOM FOR IT ALL—AND MORE!

Continued on the next page.

Experiment: From Confusion to Expanded Awareness—*continued.*

Use this sheet as your cover page. Paper clip or staple it on top of the other four. You don't have to believe what you have written on your cover page. Just write it and keep it with the other four pages.

Review your descriptive pages of self-awareness. Share them with a friend or group that you trust. *Make a commitment to yourself to do nothing* about this so-called "confusion" for a designated amount of time—twenty-four hours, one or two weeks, six months, whatever you choose. During that time, review your awareness sheets frequently. Add to them if you like, but *take nothing away.*

After working with this experiment for a while, check to see if your experience of confusion has changed. Check to see if you are sitting in the press box, with a better view.

Many Answers (An Affirmation)

For what it might be worth to you, here is a statement of affirmation that I wrote at the suggestion of my therapist many years ago. It's still a good reminder for me now and again. Try it yourself, or better yet, write your own.

> *I am not so much confused as I am more expansive than I have habitually thought. The expanded version of me is not attached to answers in the back of the book, has a multitude of feeling responses to any given experience, and remains connected to spirit (or inner-knowledge) at all times. The expanded, self-aware me knows that for every "single" question, there are many answers.*

I am not confused. I am just right in
the middle of my experience.

16

Changing the Things You Can

The Problem: "I feel stuck. I've learned a lot, and I've successfully applied some of that information to my life. But it's one thing to sit reading a self-help book, reflecting on my life, and quite another to live effectively as a self-compassionate, self-responsible person out there . . . you know, in the real world."

The Need: There is a need for something simple and practical to help identify how you are getting stuck, and what to do about it.

The Help: It's time for a quick and easy, pocket-size guide for assessing self-responsibility.

Applying self-help material to our day to day lives can be a little like learning to ride a bicycle in interstate traffic. What we have mastered in theory, or even in practice among a safe group of supportive people, becomes a much more complex matter when we take it to the streets, so to speak. The key to riding safely in traffic is remaining focused on what we are doing, keeping a vigilant eye on our own responsibilities.

It's no big surprise that accepting responsibility for ourselves is an essential ingredient in bringing about the changes that we want in our lives.

It would be difficult to find someone to argue the point. There is a simple guideline, in the form of what is often called the *Serenity Prayer*, that can be a trusted ally in evaluating self-responsibility in our daily lives:

> *Grant me the serenity to accept the things that I cannot change,*
> *the courage to change the things that I can, and the wisdom to*
> *know the difference.*

But how do we tell the difference between the things that we cannot change and those that we can? Considering a far less-than-perfect track record in applying this simple principle, we understandably may ask, "Can I really trust my own judgment in this important matter?" A better, more productive, question to ask is, "*How can I develop good judgment* in distinguishing the difference between the things that I can and cannot change?"

I have a friend who says that we are actually very good at telling the difference between the things that we can and cannot change. According to my friend, the problem is that he we apply the serenity prayer *backwards*: pouring loads of energy into efforts to change the things we have no chance of changing, and little or no effort into the things we can. When I first heard this, I laughed at the humor intended, but as I thought about it, the backwards application of the Serenity Prayer seemed more accurate than I wanted it to be.

Towards Change

What follows are seven checkpoints that I have used in my life, and in working with others, to help determine how well we are doing in the realm of self-responsibility. To the degree that we are effectively accepting, and acting from, a position of genuine responsibility for ourselves, we will be *in motion* towards the change that we desire. These checkpoints are not intended as a way of "grading" yourself, but as a way of pinpointing problem areas, a way of locating your stuck places along the path of self-forgiveness. Post these checkpoints where you will most need to see them (above your desk, on your refrigerator, at your bedside, in the bathroom), and use them *to improve* your level of self-responsibility. Beware of the Should Monster who will attempt to use this information against you, diverting valuable energy into self-criticism.

The Seven Checkpoints

The next time you are experiencing some pain or discomfort in your life (most of us don't have to wait too long for the opportunity to present itself), identify your problem as specifically as you can, and then "try on" the seven statements that follow. As you focus on your problem (or stuck place), repeat each statement to yourself (preferably aloud), and pay close attention to the responses that you experience. Notice how your body responds: Can you relax around the statement? Do you feel powerful? Or do you feel increased tension, tightness, or other sensations in particular areas of your body? How does your stomach feel? Your chest or throat? The back of your neck? Your hands? Just be aware of your physical responses.

Notice your emotional responses: Do you feel angry or frustrated? Hurt? Powerless? Helpless? Sad? Or do you feel empowered and self-confident? Again, allow the awareness of your responses to be your goal. Awareness without immediate evaluation will provide considerably more information than the old "let's categorize everything right away" thinking ever did. Good problem solvers know that gathering information without jumping to conclusions is pivotal to arriving at successful solutions.

Listen also to your mind's responses to each of the seven statements. What do the individual members of your committee within have to say? Sit quietly and listen; you will not need to go looking for these responses. And remember: it is all just a gathering of information. Valuable information.

The better you get at this kind of nonjudgmental information gathering, the more self-responsible you will become, and the more you will find yourself stumbling into productive real-world solutions to your problems. Sometimes when we turn all the puzzle pieces up and step back to look, the solutions become obvious.

The Seven Checkpoints

1. I know that *the resolution* of my problem *lies within my reach.*

2. The *motivation* for solving my problem *is solely my responsibility.*

3. I can only change myself, and *I will take action* to do so.

4. I will *seek and accept support* for solving my problem.

5. I will recognize and *acknowledge improvement* when it occurs.

6. I will *use new behavior* where familiar behavior has been ineffective.

7. I will do whatever it takes to *remain self-compassionate and self-forgiving* all along the way.

A Pocket Manual

If this chapter has been helpful, copy the seven checkpoints on a piece of paper, put it in your pocket, purse, briefcase, or whatever. Keep the checkpoints handy. For the next week or so, refer to them often. Train yourself to think in terms of the seven checkpoints. Think of it as defensive bicycle-riding lessons. And I will see you on the interstate. Nice bike.

Journal Exercise

A Strategy for Change

Specific application: When you are feeling stuck, use the seven checkpoints to identify where you might be dropping the "self-responsibility" ball. Write about problem areas that you discover, and about specific plans to change.

General application: Write about yourself in regards to *each* checkpoint. What are your strengths? Where do you need improvement? Do any of the checkpoints that present a major challenge for you?

If you intend to make specific efforts to improve your self-responsibility, write a statement of commitment to yourself. After all, responsibility to yourself is what this is all about.

17

Confronting the Distracters

The Problem: "I can't get past the fact that I am constantly thinking about food. I feel caught in the middle of a great tug-of-war playing out in my mind and my body. I hate my physical body; in fact, I hate myself for having this ridiculous problem in the first place. Food is my best friend and my worst enemy."

Or . . .

"I'm beginning to think I may have a drinking problem. As much as I would like to convince myself that I have it under control, I can feel that control slipping away from me. I'm drinking too often, and when I get really honest with myself, I'm drinking for the wrong reasons. Without alcohol, I'm not sure I could relax at all."

Or . . .

"I don't seem to be able to stay out of a relationship. It's like I am not enough, like I am incomplete without a boyfriend. And when I do have a boyfriend, my sense of well-being hinges on how he is doing, and specifically, what he is thinking about me and our relationship. It's like I'm not in charge of my own life."

(You may be experiencing a similar dilemma with prescription medication, marijuana, other illicit drugs, or with sex, shopping, or gambling. The list can go on.)

The Need: Compulsive behaviors and/or obsessive thinking are blocking your path to self-forgiveness. You need to risk becoming vulnerable enough to take a completely honest look at this potentially very serious problem.

The Help: It's time to learn a practical model for understanding, confronting, and changing addictive and compulsive behaviors.

It would be difficult, to say the least, to work on the engine in my car without lifting the hood. Lifting the hood is a simple, but absolutely necessary part of working on the engine. And so is keeping the hood up while I work, so that it doesn't come crashing down on my head.

When addictive or compulsive behaviors are present, they are not usually, in and of themselves, the primary problem, but they certainly will block any access to that primary problem. Identifying and resolving addictive or compulsive problems is the necessary step of lifting the hood so that we will have access to our "engines," which are in need of maintenance and repair.

The only chance this metaphor has of surviving is if we assume that the hood on our car is extremely difficult—you might say, resistant—to open. Try a Stephen King twist: imagine a hood with a mind of its own, determined to remain tightly closed. Further, imagine that this bizarre hood will actually deny its existence: "I don't know what your problem is. Nothing is stopping you from working on the engine. You don't need to lift me because I'm not here."

If any of this seems a little strange, or even crazy, to you, your perceptive abilities are intact. Welcome to the world of addiction.

Defining Addiction

For the purposes of this chapter, I want to focus on addiction in the behavioral sense. We will leave the medical definition for another time, perhaps another book. In its simplest terms, an addiction exists when a particular voluntary behavior (or series of behaviors) results in more negative consequences than positive, and the behavior persists in spite of those negative consequences. This can even be stated mathematically:

Negative consequence $\longrightarrow$

Positive benefit + Behavior continues = Addiction.

Alcoholism

The classic example, of course, is alcoholism. Alcoholics find themselves with a reduced capacity to predict, or control, their own behaviors in the presence of alcohol. This may manifest itself simply as someone drinking more than he or she had intended, or reversing a decision to abstain from alcohol when faced with an opportunity to drink. The alcoholic is likely to undergo at least some personality change when drinking, and sometimes may think and act drastically different when under the influence.

If you are addressing the possibility of an alcohol problem, it is very important that you not fall prey to stereotypical images of "the alcoholic." For example, "I can't be an alcoholic because . . . I don't drink in the mornings, I don't drink alone, I hold down a good job and remain a reliable worker, I have never had a DUI (or DWI), I don't have to drink every day, I don't get drunk every time I drink, I only drink beer (or wine) . . ." Instead of defensively focusing on the problems you have not experienced, make a list of what you consider to be negative experiences you have had that you believe were either caused by, or complicated by, your use of alcohol. Consider your list of consequences not only in terms of frequency, but also of intensity or importance and of predictability ("Am I able to predict accurately what will happen when I use alcohol?").

Other Addictions

Now, apply the preceding discussion about alcoholism to any other mood-altering chemical. Next, replace alcohol and drug use with any of the following:

- Overeating

- Undereating (restricting food intake, and/or use of laxatives, self-induced vomiting, or excessive exercise to "get rid of" food ingested)

- Compulsive need for sex

- Desperate need to be in a relationship

- Compulsive spending, shopping, gambling, or working

- Compulsive need to be "in control"

Plug any of the above into our equation (Negative consequence $\longrightarrow$ Positive benefit + Behavior continues = Addiction), and there you have it. Certainly, you need to consider the severity of the addiction or compulsion when devising a plan to resolve the problem. It is important to match the level of treatment with the severity of the problem. If the hood of my car is stuck because of a fender bender I had yesterday, I shouldn't try to find the biggest crowbar I can to pry it open; I might do more damage with the crowbar than I did originally in the accident.

In the same way, if I choose an intervention that is not up to, or not appropriate for, the task, the problem remains. Later in this chapter, we will look more specifically at treatment choices for addictive behaviors;

stay tuned. In the meantime, let's take a good look at exactly how addiction comes between us and self-forgiveness.

Journal Exercise

Addictive Behaviors

Make some specific notes about any behaviors you are presently concerned might be addictive. What scares you the most about this possibility?

How Addiction Blocks Self-Forgiveness

In Alcoholics Anonymous, alcoholism is said to be "cunning, baffling, and powerful. "And it's true: addiction in any form is slippery and extremely resourceful. I remember a client describing his addiction like this:

> The Addict on my committee is very clever and is never short on energy. I'm pretty sure that he [the Addict] gets up every morning about forty-five minutes before I do. He works out, has some coffee, probably even reads the paper, and then he comes in to wake me up. "Wake up, little buddy. We have lots to do today."

Like the Should Monster, when there is an Addict on the committee, he, she, or it is brimming with confidence, and is always ready and willing to step in and take over. And when that happens, you can bet that a detour, well off the road to self-forgiveness, has been chosen.

Addiction can block self-forgiveness in (at least) three ways:

1. Addictive behaviors are often misdirected attempts to achieve some sort of fulfillment in our feelings about ourselves. For instance, with alcohol, the attempt might be to enhance our personalities so that we can enjoy ourselves for a little while. I had a client who was an alcoholic; he told me that with hindsight he could see that he had a higher tolerance for alcohol than did his Should Monster; so he would drink enough for his Should Monster to pass out, and then he would have a few hours all to himself.

2. Addictive behaviors automatically work to cover up, or at least to minimize, our emotions. Sometimes this is accomplished by the addictive behavior creating a "rush," or a "high," so that the less intense emotions are easily retired to the garage for storage. Sometimes, especially

with drugs and alcohol, the senses are dulled—medicated—to the point of being numb.

3. The consequences—small, medium, and large—associated with addictive behaviors act as brush fires, distracting us from the more important matters in our emotional lives. Especially if we feel undeserving and bad about ourselves, having to deal with the specific consequences of addictive behavior is not only preferable to facing these deeper, negative feelings, but also the negative consequences provide confirmation for the negative thoughts and feelings we harbor for ourselves. In this way, the addictive behavior activates a critical "should" response that I refer to as the "I told you so within." There is a strange comfort that comes from this kind of negative validation, and when we are seduced by that comfort, the result is motivational inertia.

Out of the Frying Pan

The bottom line effect of addiction is loss of contact with ourselves; and the longer we are out of touch, the more reason we seem to have to avoid a reunion. Anyone who has ever fallen behind in paying bills, returning phone calls, washing dishes, whatever, knows that avoidance begets avoidance. In the same way, addictive behavior begets addictive behavior. It's not exactly a circle; it's more of a spiral, spinning steadily downward.

If you are trapped in that spiral—near the top, in the middle, or approaching the bottom—there is no "good" time to intervene. In my work with various brands of addicts through the years, I have always told them: *Addicts must learn to quit while they are behind.*

> Addicts must learn to quit while they are behind.

If you determine that you are caught somewhere inside this destructive downward spiral, and you intend to break out, the first thing you need to know is that before you can feel better, you must become willing to feel worse. When you make a decision to separate from addictive behavior, you are making a decision to step out of the frying pan and into the fire.

The good news is that this is a cleansing and purifying fire that (if you continue to do what it takes to withstand the heat) will leave you not burned, but restored. If this reads a little like a testimonial, I'm not surprised: I am telling you from both my professional and personal experience that the discomfort, and even the pain, that must be encountered in order to separate from an addiction is well worth it. There is no self-compassion within the downward spiral; it cannot exist there because, if for no other reason, self-compassion cannot survive dishonesty. For addiction, dishonesty is a requirement.

They Told Him So

Paul is a client who had been referred to me by an aftercare counselor in a residential addiction treatment center. The treatment team at the center recommended that Paul attend several AA meetings each week in addition to seeing me for regularly scheduled psychotherapy sessions. This had been his second residential treatment for chemical abuse problems, and when I first met with Paul, he was attending the prescribed AA meetings and appeared to be quite motivated to begin therapy. He identified several concerns other than alcoholism recovery that he wished to address during our time together. He told me that he was staying sober, using no alcohol or other mood-altering chemicals, and appeared comfortable with his current schedule of AA meetings.

During my third session with Paul, I noticed some ambivalence from him about identifying himself as an alcoholic. When I asked a few questions about this, I discovered that during both of Paul's residential treatment stays, he had experienced something that I have come to believe happens far too often in specialized addiction treatment centers. The treatment professionals had taken a thorough history of his drug and alcohol use, and had evaluated him thoroughly via formal psychological testing, and more informally over the course of his time in each program via one-on-one and group counseling sessions. Based on their evaluations, the treatment professionals had diagnosed Paul as chemically dependent, and told him that consequently he would not be able to successfully use alcohol or any mood-altering chemical in moderation. Paul, not being one to argue, eventually took this information in stride, agreeing to not drink or use drugs and to go to his twelve-step support meetings. There was plenty of positive support in each of the treatment centers—from staff and fellow patients—for these decisions, and Paul actually felt very good about his treatment experiences. I have no doubt that he looked the part of a successful outcome at the time of each of his discharges.

The problem is this: each time, *the treatment professionals decided* that Paul was an addict, and then *they told him* the news. Apparently no one asked Paul—at least not with enough genuine curiosity—what he thought about his relationship with drugs and alcohol. Because of his rather quiet, passive personality style, being told that he was chemically dependent did not bring out any major rebellion or objection from him. He listened politely, and continued to follow the guidelines of the treatment programs.

But, when Paul and I were sitting in my office beginning his "aftercare" psychotherapy, he remained undecided about whether he considered himself to be addicted or not. He had definitely been told that he was, but no one had guided him through his own assessment of his problems so that he could make up his own mind. Paul was quiet and passive, but he wasn't stupid or gullible, and he had not necessarily agreed with his diagnosis, especially when he got away from the treatment centers and thought about it on his own.

Evaluating Yourself

When I conduct professional training seminars for addiction treatment professionals, I always tell them this: "Don't ever forget that as clinicians and experts, what we think about the client's condition is ultimately irrelevant." I go on to explain that, of course, "what we have to contribute via evaluation and treatment has value, but that that value is only as long lasting as the client's ability and willingness to use what we contribute. When we fall into the trap of being too self-satisfied with our own opinions, we are letting our clients down."

This thinking is true for any condition that might be diagnosed—for example, if I am diagnosed with cancer, it's up to me to decide what I will do with the information—but it is especially true when dealing with addiction because this condition has a powerful built-in security system (denial) expertly designed to keep treatment from entering the picture.

If you suspect that you may be experiencing addiction, it is imperative that you spend sufficient time and energy examining all sides of the issue, including gathering information from competent professionals, so that you can make up your own mind and make your own decisions about what you will choose to do about it.

The following is an abbreviated subjective evaluation exercise to help you get started, if you are so inclined. I will present the exercise in terms of alcohol for simplicity, but the same questions are equally applicable to any other behavior that you are concerned about.

In the Event of an Addiction

If you are concerned that you may be dealing with an addiction, the most important advice that I can offer is this: *Do not isolate yourself with your concern.* Use the preceding journal exercise to begin your own exploration of the problem, and then include someone else whom you can trust to be supportive and honest with you. You may have a friend who fills the bill, or you may feel safer consulting a professional counselor who specializes in addictive disorders. Often, this decision to talk openly with someone about your concern is the toughest part. There is something about sharing your thoughts and worries with another person that can make it all seem *too real*, as in *more real than you wish it were.*

A comprehensive procedure of what to do in the event that you decide you are the proud owner of an honest to goodness addiction is,

Journal Exercise

Examining the Addiction

Respond in writing to the following questions. Try not to overthink the questions; just write what comes to mind. And remember to make room for your committee; it's natural to have more than one point of view about something as important as this. Express yourself completely, even if that means that you need to work on this exercise over the course of several days.

- What do you consider to be the *benefits* (positive consequences) of your drinking? This is not a trick question. Be thorough in your response.

- When you think of your relationship with alcohol, would you say that you are always the one in control? Have there been times when the alcohol has been more in charge? Is there one part of you that thinks you may have a problem with alcohol, and another part that thinks you do not?

- What do you consider to be *negative consequences* that have resulted from your use of alcohol? Are there problems in your life that you believe have been complicated by your use of alcohol?

- In what ways (if any) have you attempted to change your relationship with alcohol? (For example, not drinking at certain times or in certain places, making decisions to drink less or to make better decisions when drinking, deciding to change what you drink—less hard liquor for instance—in an effort to reduce unpredictability.)

Consider all of this food (or drink) for thought.

of course, beyond the scope of this chapter, but I will offer some basic guidelines:

1. *While you are evaluating your concerns, do your best to abstain from the addictive behavior.* In the case of alcohol or other mood-altering chemicals, that would mean total abstinence, with an important exception: if you suspect that you have become physically addicted to alcohol or drugs (meaning that withdrawal could present some danger), it is imperative that you consult a medical professional who is familiar with addiction.

In the event that your addiction is in regard to food, abstaining from the addictive behavior is obviously a more complex matter. Do your best to pinpoint two or three behaviors that you know are unhealthy for you, and reduce or stop those behaviors as best you can. For instance, if you are restricting the intake of food, try developing a plan for getting at least some nutritious food in your diet each day. If you are overeating, I suggest that you focus not on reducing your intake, but on making sure that you are eating three nutritious meals each day. If you are binge-ing and purging, do your best to at least reduce the frequency of this behavior.

If you are experiencing problems associated with spending, gam-bling, sex, relationships, and so on, as above, identify two or three par-ticular behaviors related to the problem that you know are unhealthy for you, and do your best to abstain from, or at least reduce the frequency of, those behaviors during the time that you are investigating the possi-bility of addiction.

Beware of the opportunistic Should Monster lurking in the shadows, ready to criticize you if you are not successful in your attempts to stop or reduce your problem behaviors. Self-condemnation at this point only worsens the problem, contributing to the trek down the destructive spiral. If you make a plan to change a behavior that you believe might be ad-dictive and are unable to maintain that change, this is not a reflection on you as a person. It is just more information about your relationship with the behavior. Return to the journal exercise earlier in this chapter, and do some more writing.

2. *Do not isolate yourself with your self-evaluation.* It is ultimately *your* thoughts, feelings, and decisions that will count in this matter, but that does not mean that you cannot benefit from another person as a sounding board. You might need another person's guidance, or you just may need someone you can trust to witness your exploration. Somehow, having another person involved increases the ability to be objective about very personal circumstances.

At least consider seeking professional help for your evaluation. Do-ing so will not make it any less your personal assessment; you will simply be employing the services of a knowledgeable professional to help you do a more thorough job. Be conscientious in your choice of a therapist or counselor. Talk with a few of them over the phone to get a sense of how you might relate to them. Choose someone with whom you feel you can be honest and vulnerable. And never forget that in the therapeutic relationship, you are the consumer, and the therapist is the service provider. Be an intelligent consumer.

3. *Spend some time with other people who are recovering from what you are worried that you have.* (When I offer this final guideline to clients, they often dig their heels in a little.) Don't worry, if you do not have addiction, you won't catch it from anyone. It can be enlightening to sit

quietly by and listen to others who identify themselves as recovering from addictions. It's not necessary that you adopt their philosophy; you're just exposing yourself to a different point of view. (Remember the value of information gathering; practice withholding judgment until later.)

Call a local mental health center or other community agencies to ask about addiction support groups. Some of the twelve-step organizations (Alcoholics Anonymous, Overeaters Anonymous, Sexaholics Anonymous, Gamblers Anonymous) are probably listed in your local phone directory. If you don't think you'll be able to talk yourself into attending a support meeting at this stage of the game, contact the support group and ask if someone will talk with you by phone.

Find out what professionals work with the addiction you are concerned about, and find out if any of them facilitate therapy groups. Attending group therapy can be a frightening thing, especially if you have never done it before, but the experience is most often worth walking through the fear.

Two Promises

Again, from both my professional *and* personal experience: If you are dealing with an addiction, and you do not directly address the problem, it will only get worse. There is no way to predict the timing, but sooner or later, it will get worse. That is the first promise. The second promise is better.

If *you do decide* that you are one of the few, the proud, the addicted (although neither "few" nor "proud" seem particularly accurate in this context), and *you decide* that you will do whatever it takes to separate yourself from that addictive behavior, and *you decide* that you will do whatever it takes to maintain that separation, you will have raised the hood to your engine. You will have given yourself access to your inner workings so that your growth can continue. There will always be plenty more to do, but you will not have addiction blocking your path to self-forgiveness and accepting full responsibility for yourself.

18

Talking with Your Family

The Problem: "Now that I'm working hard to stop shaming myself, it seems like my family is picking up the slack. Just when I think I'm making progress in changing my beliefs about myself, they put me through a sort of brainwash refresher course. And it's very effective."

Or . . .

"In their attempts to support me, my parents are so clumsy. I believe that their intentions are good, but it's like they are always able to say just the wrong thing."

Or . . .

"My husband just doesn't get it. The more serious I've gotten about making positive change in my life—and hopefully in our lives—the more impatient, irritable, and even resentful he becomes. Whose side is he on anyway?"

The Need: There is a need to understand what makes our changing so difficult for those who are close to us. The goal is not to understand them in order to take responsibility for them, but if we can understand the nature of their resistance or their inadequate responses, we will be in a much better position to take good care of ourselves in the midst of their less-than-helpful interactions with us.

The Help: It's time for a refresher course in family dynamics. With an accurate map, we can navigate the sometimes treacherous, and often tricky, terrain of marriage and family more effectively.

========

A Family Betrayed

Think of it this way: For however many years, you have been an actor in a production that, for better or worse, has had a long run. You and the other actors have been performing the same play, two shows a day, three on weekends, day in and day out, for whatever those number of years are. Everyone knows their parts—by heart.

Now, all of a sudden, there *you* are—Act II, Scene 4—improvising! That's right, out of nowhere, whether or not the other actors have suspected that you have been playing a little close to the edge, you have junked the well-worn script, and now you are writing your own lines and inventing your own stage directions as you go along. Or maybe you are refusing to recite any lines at all.

The longer this strange behavior continues, the clearer it becomes to the other actors that this is not a temporary misstep; no, you are essentially performing your own play right there in the middle of the old one.

What will the other actors think? That's easy; they will at least think that you have lost your mind, and it is very likely that they will feel *confused* (even though that's not really a feeling according to whoever wrote chapter 16), and maybe even *betrayed*.

This is not so much a matter of who is right and who is wrong, as it is a study in what happens when one part of a well-established larger system changes. The classic image for this is a mobile, those colorful toys we hang over the crib to keep the baby entertained. No part of the mobile is without influence on the others. When any one part moves, so does the rest of the mobile. Families are like those mobiles in that, through their spoken and unspoken rules of communication and assignment of roles, everyone is connected to the whole.

For instance, I have worked with many individuals and families who have lived with an unspoken commandment of "thou shalt not be angry." Anger, in these families, is considered to be the opposite of love, or as one client explained, " [In my family] anger is synonymous with betrayal." Ironically, families with this policy of zero tolerance for anger will tend to have an entire garage, with some additional rented storage space, full of anger. Since the unspoken commandment cannot possibly stop the normal, and necessary, human emotion of anger, what is actually not tolerated in these families is the *expression* of anger. When the family system is organized around this kind of limiting and misleading belief system, and someone (like you, for example) rocks the boat with something as bold as independent thought, the mobile moves, the family reacts.

When we are working to let go of excessive self-criticism and shame, the love, understanding, and support of family can play a powerful role. In the great majority of families, the love is not difficult to come by, while effective ways to be supportive must be learned. The feeling of love alone, or the presence of positive intention, will not automatically be communicated as support.

It is not particularly easy for family members to hear that their good intentions have not been perceived as supportive. It can be even more difficult when they hear that many of the ways they have been trying to help have actually been perceived as part of the problem. (Constant, unsolicited advice giving is a good example of this.)

Many families I have worked with have a tough time accepting the idea that in order to be effectively supportive, they will need to learn new skills in communication and be willing to behave differently in their family relationships. Depending on their own personal desire to become introspective, family members will respond with more or less frustration, feelings of inadequacy, and resentment. Resentment is common when family members—especially parents or a spouse—believe that they are being blamed for the problems. Once their defenses have been activated, it becomes difficult (or impossible) to either receive support from them, or to communicate specific needs to them. Too often, the result is a division within the family that is characterized by a sense of being greatly misunderstood and judged unfairly.

Journal Exercise

Family Reactions

What are some ways that you are afraid family members will misunderstand your efforts to make changes?

What are some specific ways that you wish (or hope) members of your family will be able and willing to support you?

Assessing Their Potential

When you can gather family support for your efforts to change, by all means, do so. Like any relationship, establishing that support may take some work, but it will be well worth your efforts if your family members are open to communicating honestly.

However, you will also need to be able to recognize a brick wall when you hit one.

Think of family support along a continuum, with one end of the continuum being *highly supportive and helpful,* and the opposite end being *highly interfering and destructive.* In order to assess where your own family's potential falls along the continuum, let's explore three categories of variables affecting that potential.

Intention

Positive intention is necessary but not sufficient for the expression of benevolent support. Sometimes parents, siblings, or spouses will assume that because they "mean well," we should accept whatever they do or say as support. Our Should Monsters will often help this expectation along by telling us that when someone "means well" we have no right to complain; we should just be grateful. But what if the "well meaning" comment or action does not feel supportive? What if it feels either neutral and impotent, or critical and counterproductive?

It is important to respect a family member's intention, but that does not preclude being aware of what we need in order to feel supported. After all, a significant part of what we want to improve as self-forgiving people is our ability to trust our own instincts and perception of needs. The family member who is willing to listen to our specific needs is the family member who is flexible enough to learn new ways to express his or her genuine positive intention.

When there is resistance to this communication about needs, the family member is probably stuck in an alternate agenda—very possibly unknown even to him or her. An alternate agenda will usually arise out of a fear of being to blame or being judged as bad or wrong. A parent, upon learning that you are seeing a therapist, or reading a book about self-forgiveness, asks, "Is it my fault? Are you having to do these things because of something I did or did not do?" This parent's question could be motivated purely by curiosity, but more than likely the not-so-hidden agenda is the parent's own need for reassurance, the need to hear, "No, it was nothing you did. It's not your fault." Another parent, with a more aggressive defense structure, will not ask about blame, but will declare, "It's not my fault." This parent will probably be pointing to flaws in the son or daughter, again in an unconscious attempt to rescue him- or herself from feeling responsible for the child's problems.

This dynamic operates in marriages too. I can testify that almost every time my wife is troubled or upset about something, my reflex is to want to know if she is upset because of something I did or did not do. I have a long history with this reflex (learned well from my father), accompanied by anger at the possibility of being falsely blamed, and guilt, whether or not I am "guilty."

Be it parent, spouse, sibling, uncle, or aunt, the need for this reassurance does not necessarily have to stand in the way of offering effective support. What will make the difference is the family member's ability and willingness to either set this need aside temporarily or to ask briefly and get the need met so that he or she can return to offering support in a way that is meaningful to you.

Knowledge

The more a family member knows about the negative effects of self-criticism and the importance of self-forgiveness, the more likely that person can be effectively supportive. Probably more important than pre-existing knowledge of the subject is the openness and willingness to learn. Remember the Zen principle of beginner's mind.

The openness and willingness to learn contributes to the interaction between the family member and you, and interactive communication (versus one-way communications such as complaining or advice giving) is almost always felt as more supportive. With interaction, the support remains personalized, and there is an opportunity for everyone concerned to continue to increase their knowledge.

Interest in Personal Growth

Recently a young man related a conversation with his father to a support group. The conversation ended abruptly when, in response to the young man's request for the father to attend a therapy session with him, the father said, "I am fifty-nine years old, and I am through changing." End of story. Door slammed. One more thing: the young man's father is a psychologist.

The third variable in assessing family members' potential for providing support is the individual family member's interest in his or her own personal growth. With a desire for self-knowledge, the family member will be more likely to be empathic to the need for support on your own terms, and will probably look upon supportive interaction as a valuable experience in and of itself. In short, family members who are invested in their own personal growth will become fellow travelers down the road less traveled, rather than well wishers waving good-bye as you move down the road.

The common denominator to all three of these variables—intention, knowledge, and interest in personal growth—is *willingness.* The supportive person is the person who is willing to listen, willing to respond to your needs, willing to be wrong, willing to learn, willing to grow, and willing to be with you and your need for support without having to have all the answers.

Talking to Them

Have you ever said—or at least thought—"If he really loved me, then I wouldn't have to tell him what I need"? Most of us have grown up with this inaccurate Hollywood lie about love—that when someone loves us, communication as we've known it becomes unnecessary. Supposedly a process similar to osmosis takes over when love sets in, and information about each other's needs begins to be transferred automatically from one to the other by absorption. Therefore, if you don't know precisely what I need, then you must not love me. What a set-up!

Here's the antidote to the Hollywood lie: When we love someone, good old-fashioned communication becomes more necessary than ever—for two very good reasons: First, the relationship is that much more valued and therefore requires more specialized care, and second, we tend to love people who "push our buttons."

This is a tricky combination, playing emotional bumper cars with the people we value the most. But that is what we do, and if we want the healthy support of the people we care about, we had better begin with an evaluation of our own ability to communicate effectively.

You may decide to talk with your parents, your siblings, your spouse, or other family members because you are beginning to learn the essential art (with just a dash of science) of self-forgiveness. Maybe you are beginning your journey, and you want the people you care about, and who care about you, to wish you well and be available to support you along the way. Or you may decide to talk with someone in your family because of some conflict between the two of you (spoken or unspoken). Maybe you want that person's support and don't feel like you are getting it, or maybe you feel put down or judged by the person. Maybe someone in your family just doesn't seem to understand what you are doing, and you want him or her to understand.

We have already discussed some guidelines for understanding, and maybe even overcoming, some kinds of family interference and resistance. Now let's do the most important part: readying ourselves for responsible communication—communication to accurately and effectively represent our needs for healthy support. Start by evaluating yourself in each of the three categories already discussed (intention, knowledge, interest in personal growth). What is good for the goose . . .

Next, check yourself in the following three additional categories:

Give Them "Fair Notice"

Beware of the assumption of "If they really care about me, they will welcome the changes I am making." Family members often are reacting to the fact that *something is changing*, rather than to the specific nature of the change.

Try to not sneak up on family members, making major changes in your communication and other behavior without warning. Demonstrate your respect for them by giving them "fair notice" that you are involved in a process of conscious change, and that some of the changes you will be making may be in relationship to them. Ask for their support, rather than expecting it, and be open to their questions and concerns. Keep in mind that a relationship is a two-way street.

For instance, I might make a special effort to tell my wife, my business partner, and my closest friends that I am challenging myself to be more direct in my communication. Practicing my new behavior then and there, I could ask them if they would be willing to support my possibly clumsy efforts as I learn to be more direct. By specifically asking for their help, I will be giving myself the best chance possible for a safe, supportive environment in which to practice my new behavior. The family and friends who are willing to listen to my request and respond affirmatively are not only less likely to be surprised or offended by my changes (no matter how clumsy), but they will probably welcome the opportunity to help.

Think about the Timing

Maggie, a client I worked with several years ago, took to the idea of self-forgiveness like a duck to water. By the time she showed up in my office, she was exhausted—emotionally, physically, and mentally—from a little over thirty-five years of faithful obedience to the lessons she had learned from her family as she grew up. I remember laughing with Maggie in one of her first sessions when she described herself as "ripe." She had been "hanging on the family tree long enough," she explained. I suggested that therapy might be the little gust of wind she needed to separate from the old rules of her family, and to begin writing *her own rules and regulations* for *her own life.*

Maggie may have been the quickest study I've ever seen when it came to letting go of negative, critical, condemning beliefs about herself. In her childhood home, women were of secondary importance to men, and little girls didn't even register on the scale. In high school, she had become fascinated with a woman teacher (probably in her mid thirties) who appeared to be strong and independent, and who openly expressed views that Maggie's father would have called "commie thinking." From what I could gather from Maggie's description, what her father would have taken for communism was in fact a positive self-esteem and strong opinions about societal discrimination against women. Maggie saw in her high-school teacher the possibility of a whole new way of viewing herself and the world. The seed was planted, and sure enough, when Maggie reached the approximate age of that teacher, that seed sprouted faster than Jack's bean stalk.

The problem that Maggie ran into was this: she became so enthu-siastic about everything she was learning—how she'd been taught such a narrow view of herself and the world around her; how her father's apparent disdain for women had interfered with her abilities to relate to men, women, and herself; and how she had never once been told that she had a right to be angry about anything—that she could not wait to call or visit her parents after therapy sessions, to "enlighten" them. But the more Maggie talked with her parents about her therapy, the more angry she became. She told me about one evening when she experienced such a "rush" of rage that before she even knew what was happening, she was across the room with her face not six inches from her father's. "Another second," she said, "and I would have had my hands around his sixty-five-year-old throat."

At Maggie's request, I spoke with her parents about their perspec-tive. They were both in their sixties, but in excellent health, and both of them impressed me as being quite intelligent. A couple of days after I met with them, I spoke with Maggie and summarized my thoughts about the session like this:

> It seems to me that your parents sincerely want to be supportive
> of your therapy, but they are—especially your mom—feeling pretty
> threatened by it right now. I think your mom has been protecting
> your dad for so long that she has no idea how not to. Your dad,
> on the other hand, seems oblivious to her protection. I think that
> he is experiencing quite a lot of guilt about what kind of a parent
> he was for you. In highly oversimplified terms, your mom is
> scared and your dad is feeling guilty. I got the sense that they
> both were at least a little angry, but there was no way either one
> of them was going to acknowledge that in the span of our one,
> short hour together. And I remember what you have told me about
> direct expression of anger being taboo in your family.
>
> Personally, I don't see anything wrong with your feeling
> responses to the work you've been doing here [in therapy] or, for
> that matter, to your recent conversations with your parents about
> your new insights. I do think that you may be doing yourself and
> them a disservice by confronting them with this information so
> quickly and so intensely. I even wonder if you might be avoiding
> some of your own feelings of hurt and sadness by rushing so
> quickly to your parents.
>
> I want you to be able to express everything you need to
> express to your parents, but I'm thinking that you may have
> better results in the long run if you can slow your processing
> down a little. Give yourself time to integrate what you are
> uncovering emotionally during your therapy sessions and during
> the times when you are writing in your journal. I believe that
> as you allow yourself the time, space, and permission to fully
> experience the feelings that have been stuffed away for so long,

you will do a considerable amount of healing even before you deal with your parents on all of this material. It's healing from the inside out, like a wound is supposed to heal.

I also believe that if you can give your parents a little more breathing room just now—and I'm not saying you should let them off the hook—they will become more available to really listening to you when the time comes. As it stands now, right, wrong, or indifferent, your parents are in a "reaction mode" to all that you have said to them, and each of them in his or her own way, will remain pretty defensive until you can back off a bit.

Maggie didn't like everything I had to say to her; I felt kind of like a coach giving an athlete an unwanted lecture about being a team player. Once she could understand that by suggesting she give her parents more room I was not invalidating her feelings or her need to talk with them directly about her childhood, she was able to let her own defenses down enough to examine the value of spending some more time with her feelings before delivering them to her parents.

Several months later, Maggie and her parents attended a series of four therapy sessions together, and all three reported a sense of making a good start to some very important and healing communication.

In my experience, Maggie's situation is fairly unusual in that most of us are not so anxious to rush right home and tell Mom and Dad what we are learning about how they misparented us—not to mention wanting to let them know how angry we are with them. However, the cautions I offered Maggie do apply to everyone. Whether you are close to your parents, have only superficial contact, or do not speak to them at all, beware of the temptation to immediately take the information and your feelings to them. Just as I told Maggie, being too quick to process it with your parents, even mentally, can interfere with your getting in touch with some deeper feelings. This is never a matter of reinforcing old rules that say "honor father and mother *just because*"; it is about being thorough in your own emotional work. And it is about learning to operate in that unfamiliar middle ground where respect, difficult feelings, and confrontation can all coexist.

Save Some for Later

Sometime shortly before Maggie ended her therapy with me, she told me something else she had learned during her work to establish supportive communication with her parents. She said, "I learned to be more conservative with my words than I had ever been before. I learned that it didn't all have to be said *right now*. I learned to save some for later."

I had not thought of it in those terms before, but as I thought about what Maggie had told me, I realized how important what she had said was. One of the great big booby traps of good communication is saying too much all at once. This becomes a particularly tempting trap when you are communicating from a backlog of unexpressed thoughts and feelings from a lifelong family history. All the more reason to slow down, take a deep breath, and think, "Concise."

When you are talking with a family member about your personal growth experiences, pay close attention to saying one thing at a time. Practice having simple agendas for these conversations. For example, "I want my mother to understand that my intention is not to get stuck on blaming her, but that I do want to be able to express my dissatisfaction or anger when I feel it." You can imagine how even a simple agenda like that can be loaded with potential distractions and booby traps; therefore, it is extremely important to remain focused on the specific agenda until you either meet the agenda or determine that it is not going to happen this time. Look for hidden passageways, but continually hone your skills of identifying brick walls when you hit them. Too often, when we hit the immovable wall in communication, we increase our word count, falling into one of the traps.

Remembering Personal Responsibility

Here's a reminder: healthy self-forgiveness does not exist without acceptance of personal responsibility. As you approach family (or friends or co-workers) with the desire for support, keep the following three checkpoints in mind:

- A relationship between adults is always a two-way street. Respect your family members' needs to move slower (in understanding what you are saying or in making specific changes in the relationship) than you might prefer. Be open to their questions and expressions of concern, keeping your own defensiveness in check; this is listening from your adult Decision Maker position. It is possible to be patient without being a wimp.

- It is essential that you be clear (with yourself) about your agenda when you open conversation with your family members. Distinguish between

   1. Conveying information about yourself that you want your family member to have

   2. Requesting specific support from a family member

   3. Expressing dissatisfaction, disappointment, anger, or resentment to a family member

- All three of these agendas are completely legitimate, but your communication will not have a chance of feeling successful unless you are honest with yourself about your agenda.

- Refer to chapter 13 about developing the Inner Parent. Especially when talking to parents, it is easy to instantly regress in emotional age when interacting with them; all of a sudden you're eight years old again, and your parents have all the power. Reinforce you primary responsibility as the parent to your inner-child before interacting with your parents about your needs and wants.

The common denominator for all three of these variables of responsible conversation—*giving fair notice, thinking about timing,* and *saving some for later*—is R-E-S-P-E-C-T. If you intend to develop supportive relationships, you must practice sitting in the driver's seat of your own conscious choices. Be the adult Decision Maker in your life and remember to stay in your own lane.

Experiment

One Sentence

The next time you are going to have a conversation with someone with whom you have a specific agenda and you are concerned about "losing you place" or becoming distracted during the conversation, try this:

Write down in one sentence what you minimally want to accomplish with the conversation. Read the sentence many times before the conversation. If the conversation will be face to face, write the sentence on a small slip of paper and put it in your pocket. If the conversation will be on the telephone, simply keep the sentence directly in front of you. Each time, you recognize that you have veered off course, remind yourself of your sentence, and get back on track.

19

Learning to Want

The Problem: "When you tell me that I deserve and can have what I want, the first stumbling block is immediately in front of me: I don't have any idea what I want. The second stumbling block, in the event that I make it past the first one, is that I don't feel like I deserve to have what I want. It seems so selfish. And just in case I do get past one and two, the third stumbling block is that I don't think I can be trusted with the power to have what I want. I'm sure I would end up hurting someone."

The Need: There is a need to distinguish between immediate gratification and the fulfillment of your deeper desires. And there is, of course, a need to find the way around, over, or through each of the three stumbling blocks.

The Help: It's time for a new understanding of what it means to want; and it's time to put that new understanding to work for you.

"I deserve everything that I want." Say that several times to yourself, slow and easy, and see what happens. Does it feel good? Do you begin to feel excited about all of life's treasures that will soon be coming your way? If so, that's wonderful. Keep saying it over and over and over.

For many of us, however, this grand statement of deservingness is first experienced as ridiculous or dangerous. Our bodies tense. Our vocal chords may even rebel, refusing to pronounce the sentence aloud. Fear and shame churn within. And the objections rush into our brains.

Try it. Repeat the sentence aloud: "I deserve everything that I want." Turn your awareness inward. See, hear, and feel your inner responses. Write the responses down, especially the objections. In this way you are the master of your computer-brain, accessing negative programming that is getting in your way. Write it all down so that you can see it in front of you. You are refusing to be ambushed.

Your objections to deserving everything that you want will be your own unique objections, but it seems that for many of us they fall into two primary categories: "I don't have any idea what I really want" and "I cannot be trusted with that kind of power."

"I don't have any idea what I really want" is the understandable result of having lived a life necessarily focused on mental, emotional, and, sometimes, physical survival. When has there been time (or permission) in such a life to consider what we want? "Want" is a luxury reserved for others—for those mysterious "normal" people.

"I cannot be trusted with that kind of power" directly results from being told or treated as if we cannot be trusted. This objection implies that *what we will want* will exclude the greatest good for others—a sort of criminal mentality. (If you are a criminal, please skip the next paragraph.)

We are not criminals. And our receiving what we want does not have to deprive others of what they want and deserve. We all deserve the time and permission (from ourselves) to stop long enough to consider what we really want in our lives. What I want is an essential part of my core, of who I am.

Practical Affirmation

I was telling a friend about a new book I was working on, a book about self-forgiveness, of all things. My friend cringed (isn't it great to have honest friends?) and said, "I hope you're not going to be writing about those namby-pamby, Stuart Smalley positive affirmations." The next day I faxed the following to my friend.

> *I give myself full and complete permission to despise those corny affirmations.*

I personally think the fact that my fax is still hanging on her office wall is testament to the power of affirmation.

Affirmations can be irritating, I'll give you that, but that's mostly when they are served with a lot of sugar. Affirmations can also be very powerful, and a practical tool in bringing about change in our lives.

The word *affirm* means quite simply, *to make firm*. If you doubt the power of words to make things firm, take just a moment to consider the negative, critical messages that have haunted you, and maybe even influenced your decision to read this book. Haven't those messages, repeated endlessly, been effective in creating problems with your self-esteem—atleast?

My first priority when working with affirmations, for myself and when working with others, is to make certain that the affirmation has a definite practical application. Positive affirmations have three specific practical applications:

1. To rehearse positive thought as a way of creating an alternative to already well-rehearsed—and often deeply entrenched—negative thought.

2. To create an alternate choice to habitual thought.

3. To act as a magnet, literally attracting, or drawing out, our subjective internal objections to changes we intend to make.

Affirmation As Rehearsal

Consider the negative should-messages that have been consistently present in your thinking over the years, the internal mutterings that have been around so much that you have grown accustomed to their noise. You may want to refer back in your journal to the Two-Column Should Monster exercise in chapter 6. Choose one—*just one*—of the negative messages that you *know* has had a definite impact on your life to date. I asked some friends, colleagues, and clients to do the same. As examples, here are some of their messages:

- "Sooner or later, I will lose."

- "I will probably just make a fool of myself."

- "I am fat and ugly."

- "When people get to know me, they leave me."

- "I am a bad person."

After you have chosen your dominant negative message, write it down, take a good look at it, and consider how you feel about it. Whether you agree or disagree, feel angry, ashamed, or something in between, one thing you will not experience in response to your chosen message is surprise or shock. This message is as familiar as the color of your eyes, or the look of your favorite pair of shoes. It is familiar because it has been well rehearsed.

Rehearsing positive thoughts is like fighting fire with fire, or sometimes I think of it as being based on the physical principle that no two objects can occupy the same space at the same time. That is, with sufficient repetition, the positive thoughts will displace the negative, and although the habitual negative thoughts may never entirely disappear, the positive can become the more familiar—and the more dominant—of the two.

Affirmation As Choice

Many of the people I have worked with do not initially consider their should messages to be negative; they think of them as *factual*, simple realism. When this is the case, positive affirmation presents a challenge to construct alternatives to long held, habitual beliefs. Often, habits—be they behavior or thought—persist because we perceive no other choices.

It's not necessary to debate the issue of whether or not a belief is positive or negative (or a simple fact) as long as you can agree that the goal is to feel better about yourself. With this in mind, you can explore various beliefs to determine which ones might be more effective in meeting the goal.

Notice while doing the "Finding Alternatives" Journal Exercise that one alternative will generally feel better than the other, and that it will not necessarily be the most positive message that feels the best. When creating positive affirmations as alternatives to negative beliefs, we tend to gravitate toward the alternatives that are *positive and have credibility*. For instance, with the last example in the exercise (*I am a bad person*), it is not likely that immediately moving to the opposite extreme (*I am a good person*) will be very helpful. In fact, making such a drastic switch might be harmful because it may feel ridiculous and literally *incredible*, which will reinforce cynicism toward the work with affirmations. The middle ground affirmation (*I have several positive characteristics*) stands a better chance of being "allowed in" because it is more likely to be perceived as at least potentially credible.

Sometimes, the best beginning is getting a foot in the door. I've worked with clients who might not be able or willing to say, "I have several positive characteristics," but will be able to accept an alternative such as, "I have at least one or two decent qualities." As with physical exercise, start from wherever you are. If this is your first day as a runner, don't run a five-mile course with steep hills.

By linking the alternatives to your negative messages, and *rehearsing them together*, you improve your chances of choosing a more positive thought and you succeed in introducing the knowledge that alternatives always exist. Establishing a mind-set of searching for alternatives is at least as important to your personal growth as any specific alternative positive belief.

Affirmation As Magnet

What you don't know *can* hurt you. This is definitely true in regard to internal objections to positive change. We are all full of creativity when

Journal Exercise

Finding Alternatives

Write down the should message (prominent negative belief) that you selected earlier in this chapter. Read the statement of belief several times; try reading it aloud. Then construct *two alternatives* to your belief: Write one alternative that is at least a little more positive than your original statement, and another that is extremely positive.

Here are some of my friends', colleagues', and clients' responses to this second part of the exercise:

Should Message	Alternatives
Sooner or later, I will lose.	Sometimes I might win. With persistence I will be victorious!
I will probably just make a fool of myself.	So what if I look foolish. It is important for me to take risks.
I am fat and ugly.	I am not the best judge of how I look. I am attractive; I take excellent care of myself.
When people get to know me, they leave me.	Win some, lose some. I am worth getting to know; I have long lasting relationships.
I am a bad person.	I have several positive characteristics. I am a good person.

Read through these examples and read your negative belief along with your two alternatives. What do you notice? How do you respond? Make some notes in your journal.

it comes to self-sabotage, and therefore it's very important to draw our opponents out into the open. The best way to do that is to set a trap; and the best bait for the trap? Positive affirmation.

Remember the demonstration at the beginning of this chapter, which involved repeating the sentence "I deserve everything that I want"? The objections will not be far behind. The affirmation acts as a magnet, attracting the objections. The more you repeat the affirmation, the more objections (when they exist) will show up.

The most powerful way to write affirmations (so that they will be irresistible to your objections) is to write them in the present tense as if they are already true. Some affirmations that you will write *are* already true (such as, "I am a good and decent person"; "I have what it takes to succeed"), and your work will be to create the awareness of that truth. Other affirmations will not be true when you write them. For instance, if you are beginning an exercise program to improve your physical condition, the affirmation "I am energetic and physically fit" will not be true as you begin; the affirmation represents your goal. Writing it in the present tense empowers the statement with a belief that your goal will be reached.

> Most good affirmations begin as outright lies.

When you have completed the next Journal Exercise, you will have rehearsed your positive affirmation via the left-hand column *and* in the right hand column you will have what amounts to a printout of the current objections that stand in your way. The objections will fall into this trap every time. The positive affirmation is bait they cannot resist. The result is more information for you. And information is power.

The Depth of Wanting

There is nothing wrong with wanting. However, we may run into difficulties with *how* we go about getting what we want. For example: There is absolutely nothing wrong with wanting a relaxed peace of mind, or confidence in social situations, but there will be problems if I attempt to achieve these goals with alcohol or other drugs. Also, there is nothing wrong with my wanting to feel accepted, but I have experienced great difficulty when I have decided that in order to *be accepted*, I needed a particular person's (or a particular group's) approval. Double check to see if what you think you want is not, in fact, only a means to an end. If it seems so, search for the deeper desire.

I used to think that I wanted to write a best-selling book, almost more than anything. While a best-seller would be nice, I have realized that what I want has more to do with what I imagine that best-seller would bring me; namely, the freedom to choose how I will live my life. Does that mean that I no longer *want* a best-seller? Of course not. What it does mean is that *what we want* can be viewed at different levels, and the deeper the level, the more substantial the information is likely to be. Learning to track our wants to the deeper levels affords us an increased

Journal Exercise

Objection!

Write a positive affirmation that reflects something you want to be, or something you want to accomplish. For example, "I am an excellent therapist," "I have all the money I need and want," "I am a decent, caring, and healthy person."

Divide a page in your journal into two columns. Write your positive affirmation in the left-hand column again and again, down the entire left side of the page.

Each time you become aware of an objection from within, jot it down in the right-hand column. Then return to the left column and continue to repeatedly write your one affirmation. Keep writing until you are fairly certain that you have squeezed out all of the objections (for now).

It is a good idea to continue writing your affirmation several times beyond your last objection. Of course, use as many pages as you need to complete this exercise. Here's an example:

Affirmation	Objections
I have a healthy, loving relationship.	
I have a healthy, loving relationship.	No one will have you.
I have a healthy, loving relationship.	
I have a healthy, loving relationship.	You're too screwed up.
I have a healthy, loving relationship.	
I have a healthy, loving relationship.	You don't know the first
I have a healthy, loving relationship.	thing about being in a
I have a healthy, loving relationship.	healthy relationship.
I have a healthy, loving relationship.	
I have a healthy, loving relationship.	It's too scary. Don't risk it.

ability to focus on our deeper values, and the flexibility to explore a variety of means to any given end.

Here is an example of one means to tracking wants:

I want a best-selling book. If I have a best-selling book, I will have recognition for my writing and plenty of money. (At this point, there is a fork in the road. I will get better results if I follow only one at a time. Let's follow the money.) If I have plenty of money, I will be able to take time off work without worrying about paying the bills. If I have time off work without worrying about the bills, I can relax at home, do some projects around the house, and complete some of my favorite writing projects. (A three-pronged fork. Let's follow the projects around the house.) If I have time to do some projects around the house, I will feel more of a balance in my life. (Now we are getting somewhere.)

So, following only one trail, the *want* for something material has been expressed as a desire for a particular quality in life: balance. Having taken the other paths in my own explorations, I can tell you that following the "favorite writing projects" soon leads to a want to *balance* my writing work by including some fiction projects. Follow that a little farther, and once again, the material becomes a desire for particular qualities of life; in this case, the desire to spend time with my imagination, creating for the fun of it. So the qualities are fun and creativity.

This technique is like taking a trip off the main highways and interstates, without a map, deciding where to turn only when you get to the intersection, crossing bridges only when you come to them. It is an excellent way to get to know yourself better. In the example above, tracking down not so very far, I have identified three qualities of life that are especially valuable to me: balance, fun, and creativity.

Maybe you know exactly what you want, or maybe not. Either way, practice the techniques described in this chapter to build your *want-power*; that is, the power to know what you want, and the ever increasing ability to successfully fulfill your desires. Give yourself permission to explore, to experiment. Don't let the objections stop you. Flush them out into the open; look them in the eye. Walk around, over, or straight through them— your objections will have only as much power as you give them. Don't give it to them. I suggest that you invest your power elsewhere; invest in *what you want*.

Journal Exercise

Tracking Your Wants

Using the technique demonstrated in the example above, practice tracking your *wants* to deeper levels. Keep in mind that there will never be *one right answer* to something like this; there are an infinite number of paths into your psyche. And this exercise is only one means of tracking your wants. With increasing awareness of your own depth of desire, you will discover others. Stay alert.

20

Renegotiating Your Beliefs

The Problem: "I was brought up with religious beliefs that would consider the idea of this much focus on myself to be selfish, and the idea of making self-care a top priority as blasphemous."

Or . . .

"I am in a double bind: I want to be a good person, and I believe part of that is thinking well of myself, but when I even border on positive self-esteem, I feel guilty and afraid that I will become arrogant and self-absorbed. It's as if feeling good about myself (or having things go my way) is sinful."

Or . . .

"My family wasn't particularly religious, but we did belong to a church. I still attend church, and integrating self-forgiveness with the teachings of my church is difficult for me."

The Need: There is a need to distinguish between beliefs that you choose and beliefs that you call "yours" by default; and there is a need to establish for yourself permission to explore spiritual and religious beliefs—yours and others'—and know that the beliefs you call your own are there by conscious choice.

The Help: As you stand in The Hall of the Great and Powerful Wizard of Oz, it is time to see if there is a man behind the curtain.

A Foundation of Fear

Kenneth sat in his usual place in my office; we had worked together in therapy for well over a year. Kenneth had courageously faced much of the pain of his childhood, and we had worked hard to resolve a couple of very important relationship problems in his adult life. I had seen Kenneth look scared before, but this was different. The look on his face was that of a child, not frightened, but terrified. The treacherous terrain we had come across was that of his parents' religious beliefs.

I repeated my question to him. "What did he tell you would happen if you weren't a 'good boy'?" Kenneth had been talking about the atmosphere of intimidation that characterized, in particular, his father's religious views. "It's not like we talked about it a lot, but when I was bad, it was always there in my Dad's eyes," Kenneth had said. "There were always the two threats lurking: what he was going to do to me, and what HE was going to do to me."

I already knew much of what his Dad would do to Kenneth when he had been so-called "bad," and it didn't have anything to do with whether Kenneth was good or bad, or bright orange for that matter. His father's extreme mood swings were very likely the result of an unrecognized, and therefore untreated, psychiatric condition.

"What did your Dad tell you would happen to you if you were bad in God's eyes?" I asked a third time, as gently as I could. For all practical purposes, I was no longer talking only with a forty-four-year-old successful attorney; the expression of a terrified eight-year-old child was coming and going from his face.

"It's difficult to describe," Kenneth began, "and I can't be sure exactly what parts he actually told me, and what parts my imagination filled in. My imagination was definitely active on this one."

I encouraged him to simply describe what he believed (as a child) God might do to him if he wasn't "good." Here is some of what Kenneth said:

> First, I considered myself to be "bad." I cannot recall thinking otherwise. It was like the possibility of being judged as "good," when the time came, was one in a million. The threat of "if I was bad" automatically translated in my mind to "since I am bad." I still feel that way sometimes.
>
> I was told that if I was not good I would be cast into darkness for all eternity. It was more than I could comprehend as a child, but I knew that being cast into darkness meant being com- pletely alone. And I knew that eternity meant forever. I imagined (I don't think anyone told me this part directly) the darkness to be an infinite, bottomless pit. And of course, absolutely no light.
>
> As I think about it now as an adult, I recognize that I was being told that everyone and everything familiar to me could be

ripped away at any time. And I would be left all alone in the total
darkness with no one and nothing to hold on to. Well, I guess
we've gotten to the bottom of that childhood fear of darkness, huh?
(Kenneth had an excellent sense of humor. Sometimes he
worried that he used it too much to distract from his
emotional pain. I think that his humor has served him well.)

Of course, we had gotten to the bottom of a lot more than a childhood fear of the darkness. We had discovered a massive portion of the
foundation for a life lived in fear.

Kenneth is not the Lone Ranger; he has plenty of company. However,
often those of us brought up in the literal fear of God do not know about
each other, because part of the teaching (or "programming") is to accept
"The Truth" on faith. All too often this translates to "there is no room
for doubt or imperfection among the righteous."

I cannot count the number of times the issue of parents' or grandparents' religious beliefs have eventually come to the surface during the
course of psychotherapy. Seldom will the issue be any part of a client's
presenting problem. It usually does not occur to us to rethink our religious
experiences and beliefs as a part of improving mental and emotional
health. Often, we split from those beliefs in an attempt to forget that
they are there, or to at least minimize their importance, but that is far
from deciding to consider them for reexamination and possible revision.

And so we read self-help books, find support groups, go to seminars
and psychotherapy, all to help us solve life's tough problems, and ultimately to learn to feel good about ourselves.

Think of it this way: You decide that your house needs work, and
you set out to renovate and redecorate. Having done so, at considerable
effort and expense, the place is looking much better. You feel good about
the work you have done . . . until you notice that hairline crack crawling
up the living-room wall. A closer inspection reveals more problems—more
cracks and floors that are uneven. There are problems with the basic
structure of the building that you call home. The diagnosis: you have
structural damage in the foundation.

Deeply entrenched religious beliefs that create and reinforce fear—
even terror—are serious problems to your foundation. And like the foundation problems with a house, you can ignore them for a while, but
sooner or later, they will damage the beautiful renovations you are so
proud of.

Put very simply, it is going to be pretty difficult to feel forgiveness
and compassion for yourself if down deep inside you believe that at the
spiritual level, you are probably doomed.

How much of what you believe do you believe?

Journal Exercise

Religious and Spiritual Beliefs

Make a list of religious or spiritual beliefs you were taught as a child that you question, or disagree with, today. Make some notes about any conflicts that you experience around these beliefs.

Permission for the Three Ds

Often the problem presented by inherited religious beliefs is not so much the beliefs themselves, as it is the rigid packaging they come in. The antidote for rigidity is flexibility—permission to explore and wonder and question.

Marlene is a client who describes her work in this area as "cleaning up the beliefs." She has developed a healthy "don't throw the baby out with the bath water" approach that has allowed her to hold on to some of the religious beliefs she grew up with, and discard some others. By giving herself permission (which was a big risk for her as she began this work) to do some reading about other belief systems, and to talk with other people, including several clergy, Marlene has been able to revise her personal beliefs about God and Spirit and *The Bible*. Her present beliefs do bear a striking resemblance to the beliefs that she learned from her parents and from church when she was growing up, but there are some significant differences. Most importantly, Marlene's current beliefs are hers by conscious choice.

During one of Marlene's therapy sessions, she and I came up with what we called *permission for the three Ds*. The first of these is permission to *doubt*. Like many others I have talked with, Marlene was initially afraid that the skeptical thoughts she developed as an adult could, in and of themselves, reserve her a piping hot place below. By first allowing her to fully express this fear, she became willing to take what she considered to be an acceptable—but still scary—risk. She made arrangements to meet with three different ministers of local churches. Her agenda was to ask about the role of doubt in religious belief (in this case, Christianity). To her great surprise, three out of three of the ministers supported a person's understandable—"quite human"—tendency to doubt; and even better, two out of the three actually encouraged doubt, one saying that "through questioning and doubting, we learn, and have the opportunity to deepen our faith."

The second of our Ds is permission to *disagree*. Previously, disagreeing with any of the fundamental beliefs of Marlene's parents' church would be blasphemy. Marlene continued to meet with one of the ministers she had met while exploring doubt, and her conversations with him helped considerably with the second *D*. As she read more books and relevant articles, and even found a women's spirituality group to attend once a week, Marlene was becoming much more knowledgeable about the variety of beliefs—even within her own religion. She told me in one session that it would be impossible (in her opinion) for there not to be permission to disagree, since disagreement was rampant among all of the people and books she was encountering. She joked, "Maybe my parents are the only ones going to heaven."

Finally, there is permission to *decide*. This permission is the cornerstone of self-respect. Giving ourselves permission—and holding ourselves responsible—to consciously and thoughtfully decide for ourselves what we believe is how we distinguish ourselves as individual, adult human beings. Unfortunately religious belief systems that view humanity as fundamentally bad, interfere with the development of trust in our own decision-making abilities. Religious doctrine is drilled into us to "save us from ourselves." This approach hardly fosters faith in ourselves as decision makers.

Marlene was greatly influenced by the wide range of belief systems she encountered. She was especially interested in the minor differences among believers within one general belief system. By way of those minor differences, she could see flexibility and open-mindedness. These discoveries became models for Marlene as she began to make her own decisions about what she believed.

Making our own good decisions, and making our own dumb mistakes, are essential to the development of a positive and credible self-esteem. This is no less true—and maybe more so—when it comes to the realm of religion and spirituality.

> Decisions that later seem to be mistakes
> are not necessarily wrong or bad decisions.

The Source of Permission

A workshop participant asked me, "What makes you think that this permission is ours to give?" I responded, "I'm just guessing."

Of course, this was my attempt at humor, but in a way it was a sincere answer. Who am I—or who are you—to claim to know how this massive universe of ours works? Part of trusting ourselves to make our own decisions is trusting our guesses. To do that, we have to let go of that pesky need to always be right; we have to give ourselves room to explore the possibilities; and we have to humble ourselves by remembering that *no one*—including ourselves—has *the* pre-packaged answer.

Journal Exercise

Religious and Spiritual Questions

What are some of the religious or spiritual questions about which you would like to ask other people's opinions?

Who would you like to talk with about religious and spiritual beliefs? (You may name specific people, or be more general—for example, a minister or rabbi, other people who have felt confused and scared about this subject.)

I don't think there are many of us who have not wished that someone else, or something else, would make some important decisions for us. In a way, we want the permission (and the responsibility) to reside somewhere outside of us. But I don't think that it does.

What makes me think that permission is ours to give? Several days after that particular workshop, it occurred to me what a good question that was. It is one of those questions that I will keep around, and keep asking myself for a while. But here is what I think today: I have no idea if the permission is ours to give, but my experience (so far) has taught me that giving ourselves permission to doubt, disagree, and decide works. It is working for me. It is working for Marlene, and for many other people I know.

Time will tell, I suppose.

PART IV

The Spirit of
Self-Forgiveness

A Collection of Self-Helpful Essays

And we know in our hearts
We're living the rest of the dream.

—John Hiatt,
"The Rest of the Dream"

If Life Is a Game, What Position Do I Play?

Every personal growth book ever written is about self-image, and still the question persists: "Who am I?" On good days, this mystery is at the center of our existential quest. We feel good about ourselves—curious, courageous, and intelligent. It can even be fun to hop onto this psycho-spiritual roller coaster, with its ups and downs, twists and turns. Frightening *and* exhilarating. Quiet contemplation *and* a strange sort of adrenaline rush, all in one.

On the not-so-good days? Well, that's a different story. Right?

"Who am I?" can quickly turn on us. The question becomes "Who am I and why does it matter?!" or "Who the hell do I think I am?!" or "What in God's name am I doing here in the first place?!" Then: "How did I get on this damn planet and where can I get off?!" (Please feel free to fill in your own favorite existential question from hell.)

As if the mutating question is not enough, the answer comes back faster than a speeding bullet (and can feel like one): "I am nobody, nothing. At best, I am so far off course that there is no hope that I will ever get to where I am supposed to be—wherever that is." In brief, "I am a mistake." In an instant, "Who am I?" has become "I am hopeless."

Granted, this is a description of a pretty bad day, but it is a day that many of us have experienced far more often than we like to admit.

Getting in the Game

Writing and publishing my first book was one of the greatest self-image battles I have faced—so far. When the book was complete, a good friend wrote me a note that read, "Writing is a death-defying, high-wire act, and you have pulled it off."

My friend's words marked a turning point in how I perceive myself—not just as a writer (a dream since childhood) but as a human being. I keep that brief note close by to remind me . . . to remind me not so much that I fulfilled a dream, but that *I am in the game*. I have taken the Big Risk, *my* Big Risk, and it has become a sort of rite of passage into a strange new world of genuine self-responsibility.

I am learning to define myself as a work in progress. Sometimes I am a seemingly aimless work in progress, but *in progress* all the same. I am learning to gather my self-esteem chips from my efforts rather than my accomplishments.

Life is a death-defying high-wire act, and I am pulling it off.

Playing the Game

They say that it's not winning or losing, but how we play the game. Cliché or not, *they* are right about this one.

When we can step into each new day with the maintenance of our personal integrity as our number one priority, the answer (or answers) to the "Who am I?" question won't be far behind.

What is *your* Big Risk? Have you taken it yet? Are you on the very edge of the diving board? Come on in, the water varies greatly! Definitely no guarantees.

Maybe you're not so sure; The questions keep popping up. "Who are you?" "Does it matter?" And, "What in God's name are you doing here in the first place?"

Here are the answers: "Whoever you choose to be." "Yes." And, "That is for God to know, and you to find out."

Come on in. Put yourself in the game, sport. And don't forget your helmet.

Daily Decision

Any good self-help book will tell us that self-love is the key—the key to a positive self-image, the key to happiness, and for our purposes, the key to self-forgiveness. Most self-help books convey that message clearly. They vary, however, in how well they teach the reader *how* to practice self-love. We read the book, experience the author's enthusiasm, which triggers some of our own enthusiasm, and we say, "Yes, self-love is the key." And we make a positive decision to be more loving to ourselves.

Two weeks later we have forgotten the book, and we feel essentially the same about ourselves: no real change.

There is nothing wrong with this "enthusiasm rush," the inspiration that we experience when we read these books and listen to these audio-tapes. In fact, that inspiration is necessary for our growth. But if we are serious about learning to love and respect ourselves, we will need more; specifically, we will need a personal commitment to action. No amount of insight and understanding alone will make our lives any better. We must be willing to do the legwork, to do whatever it takes to make change happen.

We each have the responsibility to seek tangible, practical tools for improving our ability and our willingness to be self-caring adults. There is an endless supply of such imaginative tools, and what works for me may not work as well—or at all—for you. And yet, as unique as we each are, there is *something that I believe can make an important difference for us all*—something that can make the difference between recognizing self-help material as potentially helpful and the down-to-earth application of the material to our lives.

That difference is made by the practice of *daily decision*. As I've said before, practice makes . . . practice. I'm not referring to the kind of practice that makes perfect. Perfect is not an option here. If we think it is—or if we believe that it is supposed to be—we will remain stuck in negative self-image and self-criticism . . . criticism that does anything but motivate us toward positive change.

To practice daily decision means to understand that changing well-rehearsed, lifelong patterns of thinking and behavior is not based on any one-time decision, as in: "Oh, I get it. I've been mean to myself for forty years. Okay, I'll stop now." If a one-time decision would do the trick, if insight into our condition alone would make the changes we desire, I doubt seriously that anyone would bother reading this book, or for that matter, that I would have written it.

Daily decision in the recovery of positive self-esteem is the equivalent of Alcoholics Anonymous' concept of "one day at a time." For the recovering alcoholic, the decision not to drink and the decision to live a healthy and responsible life beyond abstinence is made *every morning* of *every day*. The decision to practice self-compassion must be made in the same way. And in making that decision each morning of each day, we are committing ourselves to doing whatever it takes (AA calls it "becoming willing to go to any lengths") to make the changes that we desire—small, medium, and large.

In an ideal world, self-compassion would be our nature, and in fact, it is our nature at the soul level. Unfortunately, in the world of our imperfect personalities, the products of our far-less-than-perfect families (and culture), what has seemingly become natural, our *second nature*, is self-criticism, even self-condemnation, and an abiding belief in a dangerous double standard that in essence says, "Everyone else deserves a break, but I don't."

The daily practice of consciously deciding to live in a way that runs counter to automatic self-critical thinking is the essential beginning to applying any self-help material to our real lives. Sometimes the commitment to daily decision means commitment to a *moment-to-moment decision*. Moving against the current of the well-rehearsed, critical self-talk that we have grown so used to is very hard work, and puts our decision to be on our own side to the test again and again.

As in AA, to be practiced effectively, self-compassion must be practiced one day at a time—*for as long as it takes* to rehearse new behaviors and new thoughts, until we can return to our essential nature, our first nature: *Self-Love*

A Recipe for Self-Esteem

Just what is this thing called self-esteem? According to my well-worn paperback *Oxford American Dictionary*, *self* means the person as an individual, or a person's special nature. *Esteem*, according to the same paperback, means to think highly of, to have a favorable opinion of; or to respect.

Sounds good to me: *to think well of my individual, personal nature.* Or I could have just looked up *self-esteem.* It's right here on page 824 of my dictionary. There I go again, turning another simple task into a complex ordeal; what kind of an idio—*Oh, no you don't. I'm not falling for that again.*

I want self-esteem. I am even told that I need self-esteem, that all of us need self-esteem. I want to *think highly* of my own *unique personal nature.* Of course, I don't want to think so highly of myself that I forget to think highly of others. I don't want to form a favorable opinion of myself by feeling superior to someone else. I don't want to think well of myself when I don't deserve it; but I do want to genuinely appreciate myself; I want to be inclined to give myself the benefit of the doubt.

I think I know what the finished product looks like. I wasn't born yesterday; I have seen people with self-esteem before. They look just like me (and you) with a few subtle differences. Their heads are held a little higher, their shoulders a little squarer, their eyes are a little clearer. They don't tend to speak in disclaimers ("I need to tell you something, but please don't misunderstand my meaning. I'm not sure I'm doing the right thing to bring this up at all, but here goes. . . . One more thing: I hope you won't be mad at me . . ."); they appear to know what they think or feel about something, and when they don't, they apparently have no problem just admitting that they don't know.

Now here is a really strange attribute of the people I suspect of having positive self-esteem: they seem to interact well with others, *and* they seem to be okay when they are alone. I have noticed that they call it *solitude,* where as I have always called it *hiding out under the covers.*

There are several more of these subtle characteristics, but you get the idea. Or maybe you haven't. If not, I'm sure it is because I'm not explaining this in a way that is at all understandable; I'm such an inarticulate flake—*nnnnooooo you don't. Caught you again, didn't I? You sneaky little should-demon.*

Apparently, some people are naturals at this self-esteem thing. Not me. If I'm going to have self-esteem, then I'm going to have to learn how to make it. I have already discovered that you can't just buy it off the rack at the local bookstore. So I have been asking the people who I suspect of having self-esteem to give me their recipes. Here is what I said to them: "Please, leave out no detail. Make no assumptions about what I already know or do not know. I want the list of ingredients, the proportions and measures, the perfect temperature for my preheated oven, everything, right down to the intuitive flick of the wrist when you stir, or blend, or fold, or whatever. Tell me please. I'm listening. You don't mind if I take notes, do you?"

Two Food Groups

First, I learned that there are two major food groups (sources) of self-esteem. They are *doing* and *being.* We need to be nourished from both sources in a more or less balanced way. Most of us experience, to one degree or another, an imbalance, weighted toward excessive reliance on the doing-esteem, with a deficit in being-esteem.

The self-esteem we gain from doing is the *conditional regard* we have for ourselves. In this arena, we define ourselves according to our performance in the various roles of life, for example, worker, spouse, parent, church member, friend, and so on. It is here that our healthy conscience operates, steering us along a relatively virtuous path by providing natural guilt signals to which we can respond in order to correct our course.

Also in doing-esteem, we experience motivation to set goals, accomplish those goals, and even master certain functions in our lives—learning over time to be the best worker, spouse, parent, and so on that we can be. Here we evaluate ourselves according to outcome and accomplishment, but we are also supposed to credit ourselves for positive intention and for our efforts. By evaluating ourselves according to *intention* and *effort* in addition to *outcome*, we never have to lose too much ground when we fall short of a goal. We can be disappointed without being devastated.

Doing-esteem works best when it is supported by a healthy amount of being-esteem. In this way, even when our efforts fall short or fail, we still experience ourselves as essentially good, well-meaning people. Without the foundation of being-esteem, when we fall short in our doing efforts, our self-esteem is in danger of total collapse. "I have failed in my attempt to do such and such," becomes "I am a failure," a global negative self-judgment far beyond the scope of what we are capable of doing or not doing.

Being-esteem is an *unconditional self-acceptance*. This positive regard is not dependent on our abilities to function well in any particular role. The being-esteem is a birthright—best characterized as the feeling we experience toward an infant, newly arrived on the planet. The infant is not required to *do anything* in order to procure unconditional acceptance.

When the two sources of self-esteem coexist, we have a baseline sense of our natural goodness, of our benevolence, with no felt need to earn self-acceptance *for who we are*. With the being-esteem solidly in place, we are in an excellent position to risk new behaviors, and even to try on new ways of defining ourselves, just as toddlers beginning to explore their world, feeling the security of their parents' love and protection, are inclined to take risks in their explorations. The very positive consequence of this combination of the two sources of self-esteem—for toddlers and adults alike—is an increased likelihood of mastery in the world of doing. It is interesting to consider the interaction between the two sources: our capabilities as Doers will be significantly enhanced by a strong positive regard for ourselves as Beings, but the reverse is not true: no matter how hard we try, we cannot strengthen unconditional positive regard for ourselves by doing more, or doing better.

A Guide to Your Personal Recipe

I learned that the precise recipe for self-esteem, while involving the general food groups of being and doing, is more a matter of personal taste—more accurately, a matter of personal need. Our recipes may have much in common, but no two will ever be exactly alike.

The recipe does not lend itself to the exactness of mathematical measurements. Instead, it is a *dash of this, a pinch of that,* and maybe a *heapin' helping* of something else. Getting the recipe *right* (to personal taste) is a matter of trial and error, definitely more art than science.

I learned one very helpful hint: Develop *your* recipe for *your* self-esteem according to *your* taste. We have a tendency to try to create a recipe that will please everyone except ourselves. Since personal taste is just that—personal, as in unique to each individual—it is impossible to please everyone else. And so, as Rick Nelson so succinctly put it, "If you can't please everyone, then you've got to please yourself."

Because of the subjective nature of recipes for self-esteem, a comprehensive recipe card for your file is not possible. But I have learned enough to offer a step-by-step procedure for getting a good start with developing your recipe.

1. Write a paragraph or two describing the current state of your self-esteem. Let this sit out at room temperature for approximately forty-eight hours. Check your paragraphs regularly during this time, reading back through them and editing to increase accuracy. Make no attempt to revise your description toward the positive at this time.

2. Following the forty-eight-hour period, think of someone you know who you believe has a good, strong self-esteem. Write another paragraph or two describing how you perceive that person's self-esteem. Do not concern yourself with anything other than your best guess at describing his or her self-esteem. *Your perception* is the key ingredient here.

Again, let these paragraphs sit out at room temperature for about forty-eight hours. Check back, review, and edit, if desired, regularly.

3. Following that forty-eight-hour period, revise your description of someone you know (step 2) to read in the first person, as if that person's self-esteem is your own. So, "He is confident and not shaken when he makes mistakes," becomes, "I am confident and not shaken when I make mistakes."

Once more, at room temperature, allow this revision to sit for forty-eight hours. Review it *frequently*, making *no additional revisions*.

4. Now, blend your paragraphs from step 1 with the most recently revised paragraphs from step 3. Do this simply by alternating one sentence from step 1, then one sentence from step 3, and so on. When you have done this, you will have a longer set of paragraphs, probably with many contradictions. Repeat the forty-eight-hour procedure with the new mixture, again, making no revisions. During this forty-eight-hour period,

make separate notes about your thoughts and feelings after each review of the mixture.

5. Set the mixture aside, and with clean utensils (pen, paper) write a paragraph or two characterizing the self-esteem you desire. It is important to write these paragraphs in the first person *and* in the *present tense*, as if your desire is already fulfilled. For example, "I would like to be comfortable with my physical appearance," is recorded as "I am comfortable with my physical appearance."

6. Immediately following step 5, make a list of behaviors and thoughts that you can practice on a daily basis that will support your "goal paragraphs." For example, "I can accept compliments from others with a 'thank you,' instead of ducking the compliments with a joke or a self-deprecating remark"; "I can consciously take at least one risk every week that I would not have previously taken."

7. The final step is absolutely essential; without it, the work you have done until now will spoil. And we all know that doesn't smell too good. Place your "goal paragraphs" and list of "things you can do ..." side by side, preferably in a place that gets plenty of sun. Stir them both at least one time daily, freely revising your "goal paragraphs," and adding to your list of things you can do to support your goals.

Do this until your "goal paragraphs" become the absolute truth, or until you die, which ever comes first.

The next time you meet someone who appears confident and in charge of their own life, step right up and say, "I really must get your recipe for that."

The Challenge of the Strong Swimmers

Contrary to popular opinion, expecting the impossible of ourselves is not motivational; It is suicidal. This is not to be confused with expecting the best of ourselves, or believing in ourselves, or even believing that we can be and do and have what we once thought impossible. In any given moment we are who we are; we have what we have. Expecting it to be different *in that moment* is certain pain. Emotional pain equals the difference between our expectation and what actually is. It's math.

I call it *The Amazing Mathematical Formula for Pain*:

What is - What I expect of myself = My level of emotional pain

"But there is nothing I can do about that," you say, "except to work harder to reach those expectations."

What about the expectations that we do reach, only to watch them immediately soar higher? Libby, a client working in group therapy described a vivid picture of this:

> *When I was growing up, we lived near the ocean, and my father taught me to swim there. I remember swimming hard to reach him as he stood waist deep in the surf, his arms extended to encourage me. The strange part is that I have absolutely no memory of ever reaching my father. What I do remember is that as I would be nearing him, almost there, he would move back to encourage me to swim farther.*

I am sure that I must have reached my dad some of the time, but that's not what stuck with me. I know my father loved me; he was a good dad. He wanted me to be a strong swimmer, and I am.

Libby *is* a strong swimmer, both literally and figuratively. She has always endured when others might quit. For this strength, she is grateful to her father (whose tough teaching methods went beyond swimming lessons). But there is a down side to this particular strength: Libby feels constantly stressed, always pushing herself toward the next goal. There is no time for rest, or fun, in between tasks. In fact, for Libby, there is no "in between" tasks; they all run together—like her swimming lessons.

Everything for Libby, and for many like her, is geared to bringing current functioning up to a higher expectation. The only thing wrong with that is the word "everything"—or words like "always" and "never." There is no balance in this picture. What many of these strong swimmers (maybe you are one of them) don't know, or at least don't give much thought to, is that the experience of stress uses valuable energy just like anything else we do, think, and feel. *And stress gets very bad gas mileage.*

Out of Balance

Most of the metaphorical strong swimmers I have known live with a steady flow of adrenaline to keep them going. Quite naturally, that can only last for so long before there is a "crash" or "burn out." When that happens, strong swimmers do not make wise use of their downtime; they generally spend it in emotional pain (remember the mathematical formula) because in their view there is no place for downtime; they simply cannot afford it. In fact, most of them are quite afraid of the quiet and the calm that comes when they are not swimming as fast as they can. These strong swimmers don't fear slowing down, or falling a little behind. They live with extremes, and they fear drowning. For them, there is no distinction between easing off and death by drowning.

Seeking Balance

The challenge for the strong swimmer—should he or she decide to accept it—is to study *The Amazing Mathematical Formula for Pain*, and to apply the math to his or her life. Here's how, in a step-by-step description (strong swimmers love step-by-step descriptions):

1. Quantify your *current level of functioning* on a scale from 1 to 10, with one being "barely functioning," and ten being "super-human functioning."

   1——2——3——4——5——6——7——8——9——10

2. Quantify your *current expectation* of functioning on the same scale.

   1——2——3——4——5——6——7——8——9——10

3. Using *The Amazing Mathematical Formula for Pain*, compute your current level of stress, or emotional pain.

   Step 2 - Step 1 = Level of Stress/Pain

4. Work to reduce the numerical answer to step 3 by (pay close attention here, swimmers) bringing your answer for step 2 in line with your answer for step 1.

That's right, reduce your stress quotient by *bringing your expectation down* to meet your current level of functioning. For most strong swimmers, this is blasphemy, but give it a try. Stick with it for a few days, even a couple of weeks, to see if you can find a way for the strong swimmers' challenge to work for you. Even though you may fear it, I promise that you will not lose your ability to endure. You may however, lose some of your willingness to endure *all* the time, *every* time.

Extra Fuel

When you take the risk of bringing your expectations in line with your present-tense reality (this, by the way, is called *acceptance*), new energy becomes available to you. This is the energy previously consumed by the stress or the pain. Once released to you, how you choose to invest that energy is an important decision. I encourage you to let the new energy sit in the bank for a while; don't rush to reinvest it. And when you do reinvest the energy, beware: it is easy enough (even reflexive) to reinvest back into the stress and the pain. After all, they are familiar.

The more difficult, and more courageous, choice is to invest that energy into something for the long haul, like establishing a daily practice of self-forgiveness.

These Uncertain Times

In no uncertain terms: life is uncertain. Haven't you noticed?

Just when it all seems to be settling in around us, just when we begin to trust the constancy, the predictability of our day-to-day lives ... Wham! Something new, and possibly not so improved, puts its foot on the edge of our boat and rocks it. And still, so many of us live with our don't-rock-the-boat philosophy, darting from hiding place to hiding place in hopes that finally we will be able to avoid the dreaded nature of life: Uncertainty.

That's right: *the nature of life*. Uncertainty is not some renegade spoiler plotting to interfere with the pleasant (and consistent) plans we have for ourselves. Uncertainty is not the foe that we must defeat in order to live happily ever after. It is not the Darth Vader to our Luke Skywalker. Uncertainty is an ingenious means to the all important end.

Think about it. What makes the difference between the successful and the unsuccessful, the purposeful and the aimless, the happy and the miserable? It is our relationship with uncertainty that will determine all of this—and (as they say in the advertising business) much, much more!

If I decide that I am out of shape, and if I decide to respond to my awareness by acknowledging the need to get into better shape and begin going to the gym three times a week, I'm not going to be surprised and offended at the exercise that awaits me at the gym. (Well, maybe I will.) But if I am, I will certainly be missing the point. And if I remain surprised, offended, or resistant in any of the multitude of other ways at which I am so adept, I can be sure that the flab that I detest will *not* be transforming into the muscle that I long for.

Consider this: What if human life is the gym, and uncertainty is the exercise? What if we are aging, increasingly flabby souls in a universe that reaches far beyond this little health club we call Earth? What if we have come here, every one of us, to get into better shape? Picture it. A crowded little gym with a bunch of out-of-shape souls running around (I suppose there is some aerobic value there) *avoiding* exercise.

Uncertainty is exercise for the soul? An ingenious means to an all important end?

Yep. At least I think so. Through our relationship with all that is uncertain in this sometimes smelly gym called Earth, we are constantly challenged to remember what is really important to us. Daily—or at least three times per week—we are faced with the opportunity to "work out" our personal value systems. Our distractibility, our tendency to lose our place, is the flab of our souls. Our genuine value system (not just expressed, but lived) is the muscle.

In these uncertain times, I think it's as good a guess as any. Of course, I can't be sure.

Making Resolutions

We are closing in on the year 2000. We are living in the future, definitely on the backside of the twentieth century. Meet George Jetson. Are you someone who makes new year's resolutions? It may not be too early to begin a list of new *millennium* resolutions.

Are you a new year's resolution cynic? I know that I am—I have discovered that resolution cynicism can be a handy way to avoid progress, at least through the really cold months.

The first of the year may well have been invented as a procrastination aid—like the drawer in my kitchen where everything I'm not sure what to do with goes. *Where does this little doo-hickey go? I don't know. Toss it in the drawer beside the phone. When am I going to begin that disciplined workout program? Toss it in the drawer beside Christmas.*

This doesn't mean that we are not sincere about the desire to set and reach our goals. We just need help. Is there something about you that you really want to change? Have you tried before? Do you have a history of success with this kind of change? Have you ever failed miserably? (That, by the way, is the most common cause of resolution cynicism.)

There is nothing new here. We've all been through it time and again. We've all succeeded (whether we admit it or not), and we've all failed. The frightening topic of this essay is *change*. And I'm not talking nickels, dimes, and quarters.

Change, as they say, *is the only constant*. Change is deniable, but inevitable. We are always changing, whether we like it or not. But how much control do we have? How much choice can we exercise about *what* we change, *when* we change, and *how* we change?

You may be familiar with the Serenity Prayer; it's a very handy little prayer. The only prayer that may be more useful is one I wrote myself. I call it the All-Purpose Prayer:

> *God, whatever the absolutely*
> *best prayer for this situation is . . .*
> *I'm praying it now.*

I also think my prayer may be the only prayer with those three dots (. . .) indicating a pause. Anyway, the Serenity Prayer goes like this:

> *God, grant me the serenity*
> *to accept the things I cannot change,*
> *the courage to change the things I can,*
> *and the wisdom to know the difference.*

The wisdom to know the difference? I have a friend who says that we definitely know the difference—we just apply our wisdom backwards: putting loads of effort into attempting to change the things we cannot (or at least to obsess about them), and little to no energy into changing the things that we can.

Doing things backwards? That sounds familiar to me. How about you?

The How Problem

Most of us are not at a loss to identify *what* we want to change about ourselves. Nor are we particularly confused about when we want to change Now will be just fine, thank you. It is the *how* question that trips us up, sometimes without our even being aware of it.

We have learned to automatically think of change in terms of *replacement*. That is, we expect (or want) to rid ourselves of one characteristic and replace it with a new one, a better one, a healthier one. What could be simpler?

Perhaps you have heard the phrase, "simple, but not easy." Well, this replacement idea is "simple, but *impossible*." It is definitely one of the things we cannot change. Or in this case, the things we cannot *exchange*.

We consistently pour good effort after bad trying to pull off some sort of transplant surgery on our personalities. But there is no such surgery. In fact, the idea of substituting one characteristic for another only serves to reinforce the denial of what we must ultimately face in order to succeed in creating genuine change.

As long as we insist on fooling ourselves into thinking that we can be rid of parts of ourselves that dissatisfy—or even hurt —us, we will remain trapped in a limited view of reality. And this limited view is a handicap that few of us will avoid confronting if we sincerely want to become the masters of our own growth.

The How Solution

If not replacement, if not transplant surgery, if (as they say in the restaurant business) there are *no substitutions*, then what?

I have a friend (same friend) who puts it this way: When you absolutely believe that you must subtract, add. Meaning: *expand* rather than *exchange*.

Identify, take aim, and confront those old patterns of thought and behavior that are interfering with your pursuit of happiness. But know this: The key to becoming the new, improved you is accepting these unwanted, dysfunctional traits for what they are—well-ingrained defense mechanisms that have become reflexes in your consciousness. Don't waste your time, energy, or self-judgment trying to uproot them. When you think that you must subtract, accept . . . then add!

Create new behaviors and new ways of thinking and *practice them* every time you recognize the old reflexes firing. Sometimes the new thoughts and behaviors will feel as strange and difficult as trying to be left-handed if you are right-handed, or vice versa. (Remember Jenny's *weird* feelings in chapter 11.) There is often the temptation to return to the welcoming comfort of what is familiar. The challenge is to make a *daily practice* of the new thinking and the new behavior, for as long as it takes for the new choices to become the familiar and comfortable ones.

The new thinking and behaving will (with practice) produce better results. As you collect these new experiences, your consciousness will naturally choose the new and improved. Your mission is to remain dedicated to what I have come to think of as the *second-level response*; that is, when you can recognize the old reflexes kicking in, you respond by following the reflex thought with *a new thought of your choice*.

The secret is to judge your success by your efforts and the sincerity of your intentions, rather than the unrealistic expectations of someone else, the world-at-large, or your Should Monster. Within this model of measurement, the awkwardness and unfamiliarity with your new and improved thoughts and behaviors can be celebrated as evidence of your growth, indicators that you are plowing ahead into uncharted territory.

And so you grow. Literally "grow"—which means to increase, to expand. No substitutions. When in doubt, add. Accepting yourself, flaws and all, and expanding your options from there—that is the resolution . . . any time of year.

Epilogue

The Moon

The moon is full once in a while.
It has that ability.

And it can be many other sizes,
depending on where it rests
in relation to the earth and the sun.

Romantic humans tend to enjoy the moon
regardless of its size or shape.
We have unconditional acceptance for the moon.

We don't even criticize the moon
when it doesn't show up at all
on a cloudy night.

The moon is constantly changing
from our perspective,
moving through natural cycles.

That is, it is constantly changing
in relation to the earth and the sun.

Actually, the moon is always full.
The moon is never really a sliver.
And half moons and crescent moons
are illusions for us to enjoy.

The moon has the ability to show its fullness to us,
and yet we don't expect it always.

Sometimes I wonder why we don't treat ourselves
with the same love and acceptance that we have
for the moon.

References

Chopra, Deepak. 1994. *The Seven Spiritual Laws of Success*. San Rafael, Calif.: Amber-Allen/New World Library.

Covey, Stephen R. 1989. *The Seven Habits of Highly Effective People*. New York: Fireside/Simon & Schuster.

Kuber-Ross, Elisabeth. 1969. *On Death and Dying*. New York: Simon & Schuster.

McKay, Matthew, and Patrick Fanning. 1992. *Self-Esteem*, Second edition. Oakland, Calif.: New Harbinger Publications.

Peale, Norman Vincent. 1952. *The Power of Positive Thinking*. New York: Prentice-Hall.

Robbins, Anthony. 1991. *Awakening the Giant Within*. New York: Fireside/Simon & Schuster.

Rutledge, Thom. 1990. *Simple Truth*. Nashville: Thom Rutledge Publishing.

More New Harbinger Titles for Personal Growth and Change

CLEAR YOUR PAST, CHANGE YOUR FUTURE

Award-winning author Lynne Finney guides you through a process of inner exploration that will let you heal old wounds and permanently change your mental programming—the core patterns of belief and behavior that limit who you are and who you can become.
Item PAST Paperback $12.95

THE POWER OF FOCUSING

Focusing teacher and innovator Anne Weiser Cornell takes you through a process of listening to your body and letting the messages that emerge lead to insights, decisions, and positive change. "An invaluable tool for serious students of the inner life." —Helen Palmer.
Item POF Paperback, $12.95

ILLUMINATING THE HEART

Authors Greg and Barbara Markway outline nine essential steps that couples can take to examine their spiritual beliefs, search for shared meaning and purpose, and reconnect to each other and the wider community.
Item LUM Paperback, $13.95

THE BODY IMAGE WORKBOOK

Offers a clinically tested program to help you transform a self-defeating negative body image into a more pleasurable, affirming relationship with your appearance. *Item IMAG Paperback, $17.95*

SELF-ESTEEM

The updated second edition offers proven cognitive techniques for assessing, improving, and maintaining your self-esteem by talking back to the self-critical voice inside you. *Item SE2 Paperback, $13.95*

THE ADDICTION WORKBOOK

Explains the facts about addiction and provides simple, step-by-step directions for working through the stages of the quitting process.
Item AWB Paperback, $17.95

Call **toll-free 1-800-748-6273** to order. Have your Visa or Mastercard number ready. Or send a check for the titles you want to New Harbinger Publications, 5674 Shattuck Avenue, Oakland, CA 94609. Include $3.80 for the first book and 75¢ for each additional book to cover shipping and handling. (California residents please include appropriate sales tax.) Allow four to six weeks for delivery.

Prices subject to change without notice.

Other New Harbinger Self-Help Titles

Ten Things Every Parent Needs to Know, $12.95
The Power of Two, $12.95
It's Not OK Anymore, $13.95
The Daily Relaxer, $12.95
The Body Image Workbook, $17.95
Living with ADD, $17.95
Taking the Anxiety Out of Taking Tests, $12.95
The Taking Charge of Menopause Workbook, $17.95
Living with Angina, $12.95
PMS: Women Tell Women How to Control Premenstrual Syndrome, $13.95
Five Weeks to Healing Stress: The Wellness Option, $17.95
Choosing to Live: How to Defeat Suicide Through Cognitive Therapy, $12.95
Why Children Misbehave and What to Do About It, $14.95
Illuminating the Heart, $13.95
When Anger Hurts Your Kids, $12.95
The Addiction Workbook, $17.95
The Mother's Survival Guide to Recovery, $12.95
The Chronic Pain Control Workbook, Second Edition, $17.95
Fibromyalgia & Chronic Myofascial Pain Syndrome, $19.95
Diagnosis and Treatment of Sociopaths, $44.95
Flying Without Fear, $12.95
Kid Cooperation: How to Stop Yelling, Nagging & Pleading and Get Kids to Cooperate, $12.95
The Stop Smoking Workbook: Your Guide to Healthy Quitting, $17.95
Conquering Carpal Tunnel Syndrome and Other Repetitive Strain Injuries, $17.95
The Tao of Conversation, $12.95
Wellness at Work: Building Resilience for Job Stress, $17.95
What Your Doctor Can't Tell You About Cosmetic Surgery, $13.95
An End to Panic: Breakthrough Techniques for Overcoming Panic Disorder, $17.95
On the Clients Path: A Manual for the Practice of Solution-Focused Therapy, $39.95
Living Without Procrastination: How to Stop Postponing Your Life, $12.95
Goodbye Mother, Hello Woman: Reweaving the Daughter Mother Relationship, $14.95
Letting Go of Anger: The 10 Most Common Anger Styles and What to Do About Them, $12.95
Messages: The Communication Skills Workbook, Second Edition, $13.95
Coping With Chronic Fatigue Syndrome: Nine Things You Can Do, $12.95
The Anxiety & Phobia Workbook, Second Edition, $17.95
Thueson's Guide to Over-the-Counter Drugs, $13.95
Natural Women's Health: A Guide to Healthy Living for Women of Any Age, $13.95
I'd Rather Be Married: Finding Your Future Spouse, $13.95
The Relaxation & Stress Reduction Workbook, Fourth Edition, $17.95
Living Without Depression & Manic Depression: A Workbook for Maintaining Mood Stability, $17.95
Belonging: A Guide to Overcoming Loneliness, $13.95
Coping With Schizophrenia: A Guide For Families, $13.95
Visualization for Change, Second Edition, $13.95
Postpartum Survival Guide, $13.95
Angry All the Time: An Emergency Guide to Anger Control, $12.95
Couple Skills: Making Your Relationship Work, $13.95
Handbook of Clinical Psychopharmacology for Therapists, $39.95
Weight Loss Through Persistence, $13.95
Post-Traumatic Stress Disorder: A Complete Treatment Guide, $39.95
Stepfamily Realities: How to Overcome Difficulties and Have a Happy Family, $13.95
The Chemotherapy Survival Guide, $11.95
Your Family/Your Self: How to Analyze Your Family System, $12.95
The Deadly Diet, Second Edition: Recovering from Anorexia & Bulimia, $13.95
Last Touch: Preparing for a Parent's Death, $11.95
Self-Esteem, Second Edition, $13.95
I Can't Get Over It, A Handbook for Trauma Survivors, Second Edition, $15.95
Concerned Intervention, When Your Loved One Won't Quit Alcohol or Drugs, $12.95
Dying of Embarrassment: Help for Social Anxiety and Social Phobia, $12.95
The Depression Workbook: Living With Depression and Manic Depression, $17.95
Prisoners of Belief: Exposing & Changing Beliefs that Control Your Life, $12.95
Men & Grief: A Guide for Men Surviving the Death of a Loved One, $13.95
When the Bough Breaks: A Helping Guide for Parents of Sexually Abused Children, $11.95
When Once Is Not Enough: Help for Obsessive Compulsives, $13.95
The Three Minute Meditator, Third Edition, $12.95
Beyond Grief: A Guide for Recovering from the Death of a Loved One, $13.95
Leader's Guide to the Relaxation & Stress Reduction Workbook, Fourth Edition, $19.95
The Divorce Book, $13.95
Hypnosis for Change: A Manual of Proven Techniques, Third Edition, $13.95
When Anger Hurts, $13.95
Lifetime Weight Control, $12.95

Call **toll free, 1-800-748-6273,** to order. Have your Visa or Mastercard number ready. Or send a check for the titles you want to New Harbinger Publications, Inc., 5674 Shattuck Ave., Oakland, CA 94609. Include $3.80 for the first book and 75¢ for each additional book, to cover shipping and handling. (California residents please include appropriate sales tax.) Allow four to six weeks for delivery.

Prices subject to change without notice.